Contents Copyright © 2023

Copying and distributing portions of this book without permission or without citing the source Is a violation of copyright. Sales of materials without permission is not permitted. To become eligible to sell this book you must become an approved Facilitator.

GLOSSARY

Text Version   Pages 3 – 19

Day 1   Pages 20 – 36

Day 2   Pages 37 – 67

Day 3   Pages 68 – 94

Day 4   Pages 95 – 129

Day 5   Pages 130 – 151

Recovery Plan – 1 Year   Pages 154 – 183

Recovery Plan – 3 Year   Pages 184 – 212

Recovery Plan – 5 Year   Pages 213 – 241

Extra Facilitator Info + How to Become a Facilitator + Authors Note   Pages 242 - 248

Welcome to Radical Recovery Peer Support!

The biggest hurdle is determining if you believe you can answer 85% of the questions. Hopefully you will receive a question list or the book a couple weeks before group begins. If that fails, there is at least a week or two between the first group session where no questions are answered, and the second session. We suggest using that time to look over the questions and determine if you can answer 85% of the questions. To earn a certificate of completion your books answers must be checked for quality and completeness.If you are reading this, you may be interested in or have been invited to participate in a Radical Recovery Peer Support group. Therefore, it is worth mentioning that the driving factor of the group is robust participation. We believe that participation increases engagement and reduces the monotony of only having the group Facilitator present material.

All participation in the group is voluntary, however in some instances a person may be mandated to participate. Even in this scenario, the person has the ability to refuse participation which may result in some other option or consequence for them. This is based on their situation and has nothing to do with the group process. Because participation is voluntary, we cannot be sure from one group to another how many people will participate, causing differences from group to group of how much material any one person will present.

Our program offers a certificate of participation and a certificate of completion. People may need a certificate to receive some benefit or to avert a consequence. To receive either certificate, a person will have different participation requirements. Only a certificate of completion will allow a participant to take the next step of becoming a group Facilitator.

Group Facilitators must be able to highly identify with the program. This means that for all the questions other than the ones labeled "how does this passage connect to…," the Facilitator must be able to answer 85% of the questions. Everyone can participate by taking turns reading the material and answering "how does this passage connect to…," but those who are unable to complete at least 85% of the questions may struggle to answer them in group which is why only those seeking a certificate of completion to become Facilitators will answer the questions during group.

While many people may participate in the group for different reasons, we encourage everyone to participate as if they are trying to earn a certificate of completion because it will make the group more dynamic and Peer Supported.

About This Program:

Radical Recovery Peer Support is a program that utilizes Peer Support to help individuals achieve wellness and personal growth. The author of the program uses first-person inspirational passages to draw parallels between concepts and recovery. The Program Involves group sessions that can be done either in-person or online.

For the group programs, we have three options. The book/group is a general wellness and personal growth group which is simply called Radical Recovery Peer Support. There is also a group with a focus on higher or continued education called "RRPS-University." RRPS-University emphasizes a crucial element of recovery is getting involved in and taking education serious as a means of achieving a better quality of life. Finally, there is a version of RRPS for Criminal-reentry called "RRPS-Liberation," which discusses developing new belief systems that will help turn our lives around after an arrest.

Over the course of five sessions each group covers important concepts like the Linear Growth Model and Parallel Recovery Concepts. It Also Focuses on the nine Recovery Fundamentals which include principles like Honesty, Trust, Acceptance, Hope, Personal Responsibility, Self-Advocacy, and others. How each group presents the concepts and fundamentals is unique.

The Linear Growth Model recognizes that while growth and recovery are not always linear, putting in effort does often lead to progress over time. Growth may appear uneven, with periods of progress and periods of struggle. However, making consistent efforts through programs like Radical Recovery Peer Support can help us move closer to our hope of achieving stability and wellness.

RRPS is a Cognitive Behavioral Therapy. It is such because the description of the Concepts and Fundamentals, as well as the person first descriptions of the recovery journey address beliefs, thoughts, and feelings commonly experienced in a specific but large audience. Each program addresses thoughts, beliefs, and feelings that held the author back and provides a solution of improving our thoughts, beliefs, and control over our feelings by getting more aligned with positive expressions of Recovery Concepts and Fundamentals.

Examples of how this is done in RRPS - Liberation include changing thoughts for people with criminal history's such as "Only my failures matter," to "I have hope even though its tougher with a record." Changing thoughts of "All probation officers are out to get me" to many of them want to help." Reduces Dichotomous thinking by encouraging the view that its not all black or white or one or the other, but that there are levels of growth on a continuum and a new start can be made at any time.

The programs also incorporate themes of Rational Emotive Therapy in the different events emphasized in each program. With more general distressing circumstances in the original RRPS, to more specific events such as educational neglect in RRPS -University, and the stigma of having a criminal record in RRPS -Liberation, to our beliefs about these issues, and the consequences for results of those beliefs. The program also employs themes of Reality Therapy in its emphasis on personal choice and personal responsibility.

The program also utilizes a wide variety of homework questions that are done outside of group (common of CBT programs) which reinforce the goals of the program. Each Passage that relates an experience based on a Concept or Fundamental usually focuses on a change in thinking that improves each outcome.

Schedule

Session one covers: an introduction to the Linear Growth Model, the Parallel Recovery Concepts, and the 9 Recovery Fundamentals.

Session two Covers: the three Parallel Recovery Concepts.

Session three covers: the first three fundamentals of Honesty, Trust, And Acceptance.

Session four covers: Hope, Personal Responsibility, and Self Advocacy.

Session five covers: Support, Purpose, and Self -actualization.

Goals

This curriculum emphasizes balanced linear growth through development of 9 Recovery Fundamentals and 3 Parallel Recovery Concepts that occur alongside each of the 9 Fundamentals. The goals of this program are based on the Fundamentals of Recovery and the Recovery Concepts and are to teach participants how to:

1. Learn the importance of and how to perform Self-Care
2. Learn to develop a Recovery Plan to take recovery to greater heights (Recovery Planning)
3. learn that while participating in recovery we are at every moment a mentor and a model of recovery behavior
4. overcome challenges, handle stressful or difficult situations and/or troubling thoughts, achieve personal growth and wellness, and live a self-directed life

Goals One, Two, and Three, represent the three Parallel Recovery Concepts of Self-Care, Recovery Planning, and Mentoring - Respectively. Goal four represents the result of successfully incorporating the 9 Recovery Fundamentals into daily life in addition to the Recovery Concepts. On a graph it looks like:

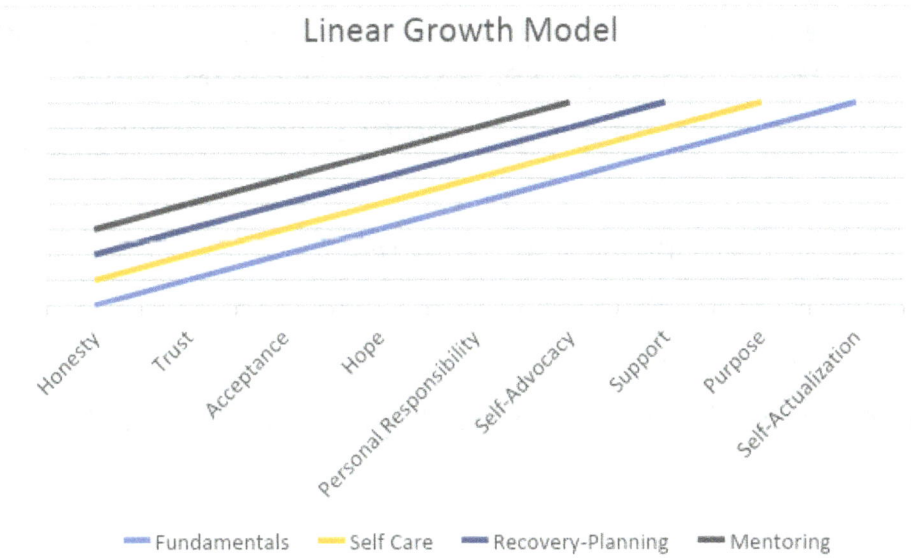

*Tip: Notice that the graph begins with linear growth along the line representing the Fundamentals of Recovery. By implementing the 3 Parallel Recovery Concepts of Self-Care, Recovery Planning, and Mentoring, outcomes and the growth line can be continuously shifted upward to higher levels of growth.

Not only does this program emphasize that every step we take along the path to personal growth and freedom is a moment that encourages others in our society, but it points out that growth is actually fuller and more complete when we remember to care for ourselves, plan for recovery, and when we help others like us, we see that recovery is possible.

From the Better Days workbook passage *'Creating Change':* "Mahatma Gandhi, the great Indian spiritual leader, said, 'Be the change you want to see in the world.' Gregorio Lewis, Author of Better Days Restates this point saying "I say that first I must change myself into the person I want to be."

The words from the passage *'Creating Change'* and Mahatma Gandhi indicate that by learning to focus on our personal experience of growth and change, the world will change in our direction, as we model the behaviors we want to see in the world.

Many programs say that **giving back** and **helping others** with the same problems as we have experienced is a sort of final step. The reasoning behind this program and in Peer Support in general is that showing recovery is possible occurs alongside every stage in the process and our actions create a lasting impact.

In addition, many people who have been successful in recovery say that

- giving back
- taking commitments to support others, and
- remembering that they are an example of recovery in their communities helped them the most in their recovery.

The 9 Fundamentals of Recovery

Recovery Fundamentals are a set of characteristics that we can use to gauge the strength of our recovery and include but are not limited to:

1. Honesty
2. Trust
3. Acceptance
4. Hope

5. Personal Responsibility
6. Self-Advocacy
7. Support
8. Purpose
9. Self-Actualization

A breakdown of the fundamentals listed first can cause difficulty with fundamentals listed last. The Fundamentals of Recovery are qualities we want to encourage in participants of this program. It is important to remember the quote from Mahatma Ghandi that we should "be the change we want to see in the world." Because we are always Mentors, it is vitally important that we demonstrate the Recovery Fundamentals because our effort, or lack of effort will impact others.

The Linear Growth Model

Growth often does not occur linearly, although many of us wish it did.

What it Usually Looks Like   Our Hopes   What it Could Look Like

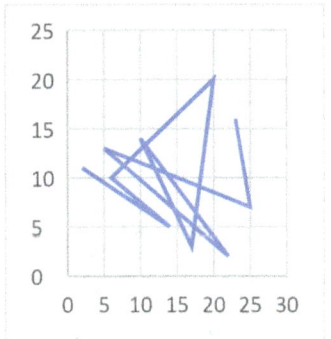 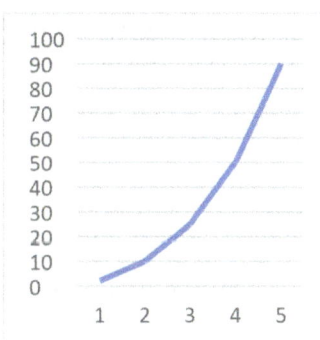 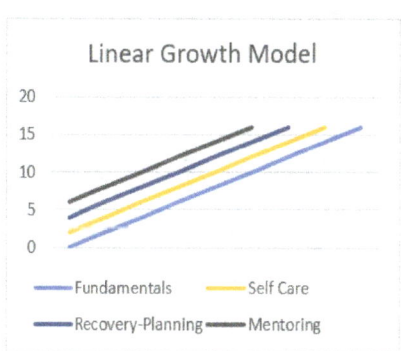

Many recovery programs emphasize that growth is non-linear. However Radical Recovery Peer Support believes that over-emphasizing the non-linear nature of growth is self-defeating. While we acknowledge growth is non-linear, we also believe that in most cases, we do make progress when we put in effort. To over emphasize the non-linear nature of growth tends to give people an excuse to use, such as that there is no guarantee that if they work hard they will grow.

With all the twists and turns and ups and downs of recovery, it can be hard to even tell if growth is occurring. By putting the same amount of effort and care into each of the Recovery Fundamentals, we will get more consistent results than if we were to put all our efforts in one Fundamental.

Because our own actions and behaviors change and impact the world around us, it is common that when we start exhibiting a better relationship with the Recovery Fundamentals, we will experience a mirror effect from the world. We may sometimes wonder why it seems we receive exaggerated reactions or displays of the Fundamentals directed back at us from society but can understand that this may be connected to our own inconsistent demonstrations of the Fundamentals.

The Linear Growth Model gets its name from the idea that

1. Growth is usually Non-Linear

2. we want to put consistent effort into each of the 9 Fundamentals which will result in more, but not all, consistent experiences in our lives.

3. When developed inconsistently with this format, inconsistent and unexpected outcomes may occur.

4. When developed in the order listed previously, each of the 9 Recovery Fundamentals assists in the cultivation and growth of the other Fundamentals.

5. When Utilizing the Parallel Recovery Concepts in conjunction with the Recovery Fundamentals, we can shift our results to a better outcome

False Sense of Security:

When we experience success at Recovery Concepts or the later Fundamentals, particularly starting with Personal Responsibility through Self-Advocacy, Support, and Purpose, we may be lulled into a false sense of security that we are doing well despite shortfalls related to the earlier Fundamentals.

We encourage that no matter our level of success with later Fundamentals, we take a look at how the earlier fundamentals show up for us. Gaps in our development may lead to blind spots that may damage our recovery.

Why We Present the Fundamentals of Recovery and the 3 Parallel Recovery Concepts in This Order

Even though Parallel Recovery Concepts occur throughout our Recovery, there are many reasons for each component that if we do not take proper care of each Recovery Fundamental and Parallel Recovery Concept, we will not unlock the full growth potential of incorporating Recovery Concepts or later Fundamentals into our lives.

We give examples of how neglecting components of the Recovery Concepts and Fundamentals of Recovery leads to a breakdown of the transition to the other components:

Recovery Concepts: This group process and other methods of Recovery can be really hard on us emotionally, mentally, and physically; therefore, it is important that we are kind to ourselves and benefit from this process. From the very beginning of an attempt to better ourselves, such as participating in this group, it will be important to maintain the Recovery Concepts of Self-Care, Recovery Planning, and Mentorship. Right from the beginning it is important to:

- Have a self-care plan, acknowledge the difficulty of this process, and create positive experiences to look forward to
- develop a Recovery plan involving the desired outcome and benefit of this process,
- and recognize that our participation in this process can either help or hinder the recovery of other participants.

Honesty: if we are in fear of what someone will find out about our secrets, harm done to others, past crimes and the things that make us feel guilt, shame, or fear of persecution, we will not know what we can trust others with.

Trust: If we cannot trust ourselves or are not aware of who we can Trust or what systems are working for us and not against us, we will have a hard time finding acceptance of our situation.

Acceptance: If we can't accept our current situation or past experiences and are constantly suffering from them or if someone or some force has an uncomfortable level of control over our lives, we will have a hard time recognizing things we can hope for.

Hope: If we don't have hope and are not propelled by our desire to achieve a hoped-for outcome, the natural inclination is to be unmotivated about our personal responsibilities. If we can't get satisfaction by working on our hopes, we often fail to develop and perform <u>personal responsibilities</u>.

Personal Responsibilities: if we are lacking in fulfilling our personal responsibilities, we often face resistance from others when we <u>self-advocate</u> for ourselves because we have less basis to show that we are capable.

Self-Advocacy: If we fail to effectively advocate for ourselves through means of showing that our capabilities or progress make us a good fit for certain endeavors, or if we advocate for ourselves for that which provides outcomes inconsistent with our recovery, or if we advocate to the wrong people, among other things, we may not get adequate <u>support</u>.

Support: A Significant outcome of working through the Fundamentals of Recovery leading up to support, is that we find ourselves in the best position to begin offering support.

It takes support to fulfil BIG goals. If we do not look for support or accept support from the right people, we will have a hard time achieving our goals. With the added effort it takes to achieve goals without support we have a hard time finding our purpose because everything feels like it is a struggle. Often, things that seem more natural or easier for us, or areas we get the most support, are also area's excellent to find <u>purpose</u>.

Purpose: Without a purpose with which to gauge our progress or put our efforts, we often feel like we are repeating a pattern that rarely changes, or that there is no perceivable pattern but rather instability or lack of focus. Finding and incorporating a purpose into our lives leads to <u>self-actualization</u>, a feeling that we are fulfilling our unique potential

Self-Actualization: This Fundamental of Recovery is often considered a final stage of development. However, to maintain this stage we must continue to put sufficient and equal amounts of effort into all the Fundamentals of Recovery. Also, the Parallel Recovery Concepts must be maintained.

What Mentors Need to Know

Self-Care:

    Self-care is any healthy & direct action we take to feel better. Sometimes we need to use Self-Care to respond to stressors, or triggering events, or when we feel like we are in crises. Self-Care that might work normally may not work as well under very difficult conditions.

*Tip for dealing with stressors: One suggestion for how to deal with especially difficult situations is to put more time and effort into the things we usually do to make us feel better.

Really good Self-Care is often planned. Planning Self-Care before we feel unwell has benefits such as having something to look forward to, or helping us not forget Self-Care. Because of this, it is often included in recovery planning.

Examples of Self-Care

- *Remembering our boundaries and what we will or will not do*
- *Spending time with family and friends*
- *Getting enough sleep*
- *Being of service to others*
- *Writing a gratitude list*
- *Taking breaks*

Stressors, burnout, vicarious trauma, poor time management, and compassion fatigue are common reasons we provide Self-Care for ourselves.

Recovery Planning:

Recovery planning is self-determined but often includes friends and family, supporters, or community leaders. Recovery planning is done with the collaboration of individuals involved and utilizes recovery capital.

A Recovery Plan

- *Is based on self-determination*
- *Identifies strengths of the individual and takes inventory of Recovery Capital*
- *Identifies goals, challenges, action steps, and date of completion*
- *May involve support from others and connection to community resources and leadership.*

In a table it looks like:

Goal	Strengths & Recovery Capital	Obstacles	Action Steps	Date of Completion
Get Masters Degree	- Have a: bachelors degree - Time: Am on Disability and am self employed - Experienced with: online courses	Classes are condensed so more is required in a shorter time.	- Clear agenda for first week - Start each day with school first - Complete all assignments before recreation	August 10th 2025

Recovery plans need to be evaluated and measured for progress. Criteria for evaluation should come from the person creating the plan and should be considered before action, if possible.

Mentoring:

Mentoring is a constant ongoing process and occurs in situations where we present both the best or worst aspects of ourselves. We never know just what kind of impact we will have on others. Remember the words of Mahatma Gandhi – "be the change you want to see in the world." One way to effect change is through Mentoring.

- Mentoring provides an opportunity to be there for a person in a way that supports them in both the best of times and the worst

- A good mentor will respect each person's unique approach to recovery

- A Mentor utilizes self-disclosure in a way that does not compete with but rather informs an individual of shared experiences

- A Mentor should be primarily focused on the person they are mentoring; only sharing about themselves or their experiences when it would be a benefit to the mentee

- Mentoring is constant and ongoing, and occurs in situations where we present both the best or worst aspects of ourselves

- We never know just what kind of impact we will have on others

Honesty:

Many of us have Baggage. In recovery, we may resist new healthy behaviors and thoughts. This may often stem from a lack of honesty about three factors, 1: that we have been hurt and/or 2: that we have hurt ourselves or others, and 3: the nature of the severity of the hurt.

It is important to acknowledge

- if we are not honest within ourselves about how we have been hurt, hurt ourselves or others, or the severity, we may repeat unfavorable experiences.

Trust:

There are different levels of trust - We can have trust in:

- a specific person or people that we trust
- in the systems we are in such as our governments, legal system, or system of wellness or therapy
- self-trust; <u>trusting that we have our own best interests in mind</u>.

Within these is determining who we can rely on, who we cannot, and what we can share with others.

*Tip – Self-disclosure: It is important to remember

- we never need to share something that would make us uncomfortable
- there is more we can share with others than something that would make us uncomfortable
- it is different to share things we want to keep private versus our hopes, goals, and stresses
- there is no guarantee what we say will remain confidential

Acceptance:

Each person is subject to different degrees of unforeseen circumstances, restrictions, rules, and regulations. For the most part, these obstacles depend on our situation, can be temporary, or can be changed with support. While we must deal with these situations while they occur, we can find ways to have hope within them and have Better Days.

*Tip – Trauma/Grief Informed: Many people will report that there are things that they cannot or will not accept. This is okay, remind them that they can still work on other Fundamentals and that there is a difference between 1: accepting that an event took place and 2: accepting an event into our lives and our space.

Hope:

If we are struggling to find hope, it will often become easier the longer we commit to recovery and through more time between distressing events. Also, <u>actively seek out inspiration</u> by:

- talking to supporters about what is giving our supporters hope
- making lists of things that give us hope
- reading recovery stories
- list their own dreams, and if possible, communicate them to someone

Personal Responsibility:

Some situations may be out of our control or cause discomfort for us. If we are having a hard time fulfilling responsibilities because of obstacles, things outside our control, or things we need or are worried about; we can ask how much control we have over these situations, and if we are doing everything we can within the control we have.

Personal Responsibility Continued -

To get back on track we can follow a Recovery Plan that involves:

- A daily plan
- A plan of things we need to do every now and then
- A plan for achieving big goals

Plans should include a way to provide for ourselves and elements of Self-Care

If we are developing a Recovery Plan, it is important to first list things we struggle with, things that need the most attention, or that create new responsibilities for us. A Recovery Plan is a way to familiarize ourselves with our objectives and requirements and decide how things need to be done.

Personal Responsibility may involve creating goals that improve our lives and our success. For information on how to help someone with their goals, refer to the section of the RRPS Mentors Guide titled Motivational Interviewing & Recovery Planning.

Self-Advocacy:

Sometimes people may feel they have lost their right or ability to advocate for themselves, or that they have lost control of their lives. Each person has the right to advocate for themselves for the same public benefits and treatment common to their society no matter what the state of their lives.

*Tip – if a person is having a hard time gaining support through self-advocacy, communicate that

- our chances of getting support increase the longer we maintain continued effort with the Recovery Fundamentals that precede this step, especially Personal Responsibility.
- we can believe in ourselves and practice advocating by making a list of goals we think will get the most support and advocating for each item on the list.

Support:

"It takes support to fulfill BIG goals. If we do not look for support or accept support from the right people, we will have a tougher time achieving our goals."

If we lack support, developing a strong support system benefits from:

- being mutually supportive to others
- doing everything within our control to maintain our personal definition of wellness
- becoming active in the community, a support group, school, or other area like employment
- having several supporters so someone will always be available, and we do not overburden anyone

Purpose:

Once we have maintained progress relevant to our interests and security, are more empowered, and have support, we may find that other people are an extension of ourselves or that we have integrated a cause into our lives.

We may also find that

- human rights,
- dignity, and
- freedom become important to us.

Self-Actualization:

Self-actualization is all about reaching the true potential of our unique selves. Once we have reached our full potential, we may find that we are freer and more capable. Often, people at this level of development begin to have a deeper connection with where they believe they fit in the universe, existence, and in relation to other people or their concept of a higher power.

In the *Allegory of the Cave* "Plato's Republic," the principal character in the story returns to people that were still "disillusioned" to help them find a better way. For most this is a natural inclination by this stage of recovery, to show others a brighter future. The Parallel Recovery Concept of Mentorship has carried many individuals' recoveries to particularly new heights. Consider the shift in the growth demonstrated in the Linear Growth Model due to the Parallel Recovery Concepts and Mentorship.

Presentation Process

The slides that can be read in the workbook or PowerPoint will be divided between all those wishing to receive a certificate of participation or completion, including participation from the facilitators. The Facilitators will start by explaining why we request full participation and the reward of either a certificate of completion or participation. The Information on participation requirements is on page two underneath the table of contents.

The Facilitators will read the first two slides of the first presentation. After that, all slides will be divided up between the participants. The exceptions to this are the slides in the first session's presentation following the slide title "Why We Present the Recovery Fundamentals and Parallel Recovery Concepts in this Order." These slides sometimes contain more than one Fundamental or Concept and there will be a different reader for each of these.

At the end of each session, the Facilitator will read the last slide that conveys information related to the upcoming session. After this, the remainder of the time will be spent on open discussion of the day's session. For session one this will be the full span of 2 hours, for the remaining session it will be the span of 3 hours.

The remaining sessions also have sections titled 'How does this passage connect or relate to the concept or fundamental.' These questions entail a short response that should connect the passage read just before this question to the Recovery Concept or Fundamental being discussed at the time. Everyone has the capability to answer these questions so everyone desiring a certificate of participation or completion will answer these including the facilitator, unless facilitator participation means some participants will not have the chance to participate.

Participation points will not be lost for these questions if there were not enough questions for everyone to get a chance to participate. A participation sheet will be provided which specifies how many participation points a person will need in each category of participation. For those who have not had a chance to answer these questions, they will have an opportunity to revisit them at the end of the group.

Sessions 2 – 5 also have many short questions. There are usually 3 questions for each passage. These are divided between all those seeking a certificate of completion and the Facilitators. These questions are not required to be answered by those seeking a certificate of participation.

The Facilitator will not participate or read unless there are fewer than 5 people attempting a certificate of completion, in which case, only participating when they have the least amount of participation compared to those seeking a certificate. Participants can choose when they would like to participate in order to get the right amount of participation points, however when some of them are close to full points, the facilitator will begin asking specific people to participate if a participant has the least amount of participation.

If participants do not have a response to a particular question, the Facilitator will step in and answer the question. If participants did not get enough participation points from this question-and-answer section, we can allow them to answer other questions from the session at the end as a revisitation.

To revisit a question requires them to have completed enough of their answers to share them and receive the required completion points. This might be useful for participants that did not complete enough of their questions before the group where the questions they did answer in the book were answered by other participants. Even if the participant did not complete a question before group, we can allow them to develop a quick answer on the spot if they are able.

Once the presentation process is over for the session, we allow the rest of the time to be open discussion starting with the facilitator asking the group if they have any questions, allowing participants to ask questions here. Next, we will do a check in, asking the group how they are doing with the concepts or fundamentals covered in the session. Once 2 hours have elapsed for session one, or three hours for all other sessions, the session is complete.

This is how the group will be Facilitated.

P.s.

On the last page of each day's session, the text will also point out what needs to be completed before the next day's session. All assignments discussed on these pages will be shared by participants in breakout rooms if the group is online, or with the person sitting next to them if done in person.

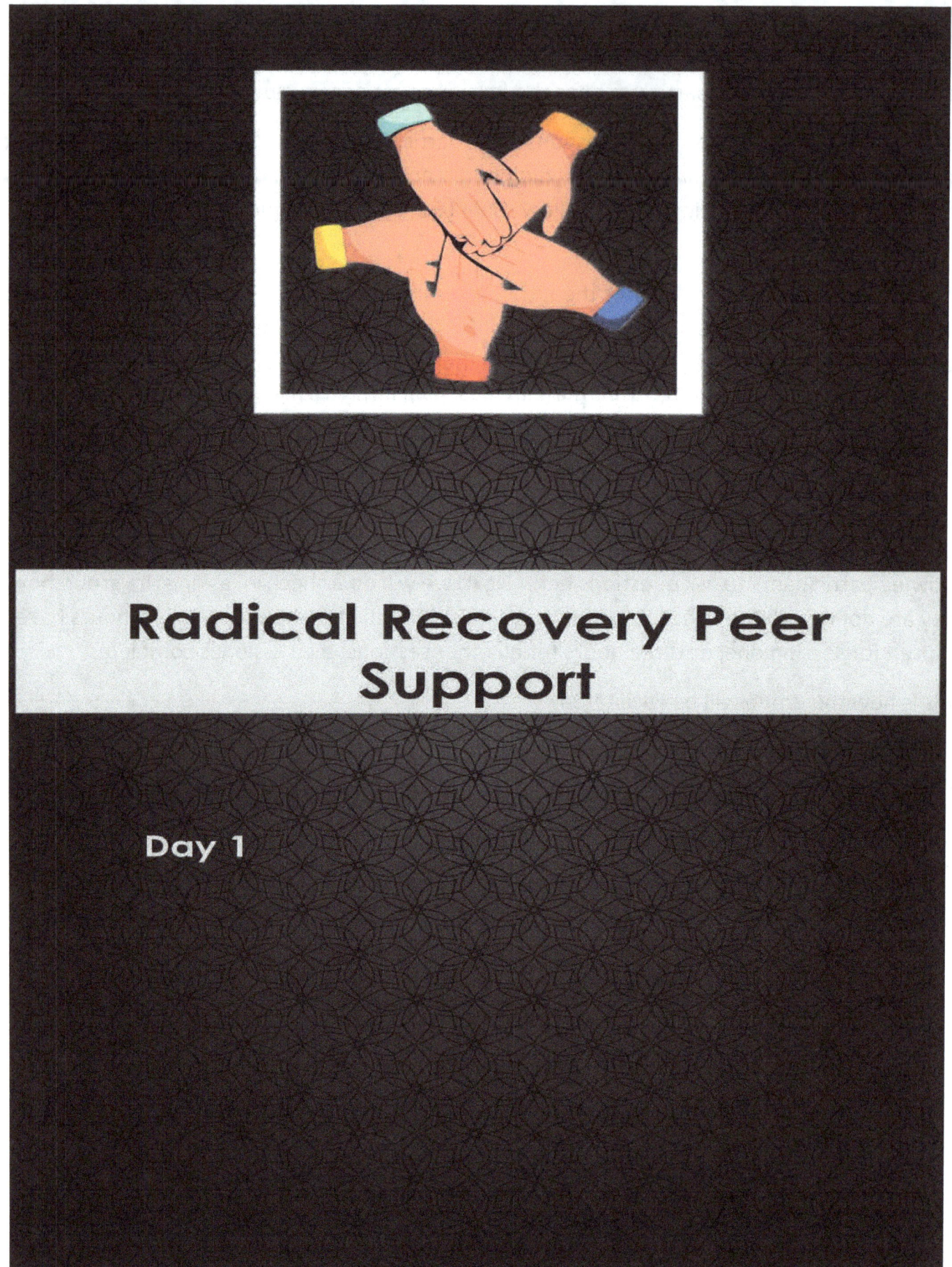

Radical Recovery Peer Support

Day 1

This curriculum emphasizes balanced linear growth through the development of 9 Recovery Fundamentals and three Parallel Recovery Concepts that occur alongside each of the 9 Fundamentals.

The goals of this program are based on the Fundamentals of Recovery and the Recovery Concepts. They are:

Learn the importance of and how to perform Self-Care

Learn to develop a Recovery Plan to take recovery to greater heights (Recovery Planning)

Overcome challenges or troubling thoughts, handle stressful or difficult situations, achieve personal growth and wellness, and live a self-directed life

Learn that while participating in recovery we are at every moment a mentor and a model of recovery behavior

From the Better Days workbook passage 'Creating Change': "Mahatma Gandhi, the great Indian spiritual leader, said, 'Be the change you want to see in the world.'

Gregorio Lewis, Author of Better Days restates this point by saying "I say that first I must change myself into the person I want to be."

The words from the passage *'Creating Change'* and Mahatma Gandhi indicate that by learning to focus on our personal experience of growth and change, the world will change in our direction, as we model the behaviors we want to see in the world.

Many programs say that **giving back** and **helping others** with the same problems as we have experienced is a sort of final step. The reasoning of this program and in Peer Support in general is that showing recovery is possible occurs alongside every stage in the process and our actions create a lasting impact.

In addition, many people who have been successful in recovery say that

- giving back
- taking commitments to support others, and
- remembering that they are an example of recovery in their communities

helped them the most in their recovery.

The 9 Recovery Fundamentals

Recovery Fundamentals are a set of characteristics that we can use to gauge the strength of our recovery and include but are not limited to:
- Honesty
- Trust
- Acceptance
- Hope
- Personal Responsibility
- Self-Advocacy
- Support
- Purpose
- Self-Actualization

A breakdown of the Fundamentals listed first can cause difficulty with the Fundamentals listed last

NOTES:

Parallel Recovery Concepts

Self Care

Recovery Planning

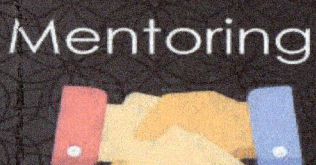

Mentoring

Growth often does not occur linearly, although many of us wish it did – Imagine if you knew X amount of effort led to Y amount of growth!

- We often hope growth would look like this

- What it usually looks like

The Linear Growth Model

Growth we can aim for

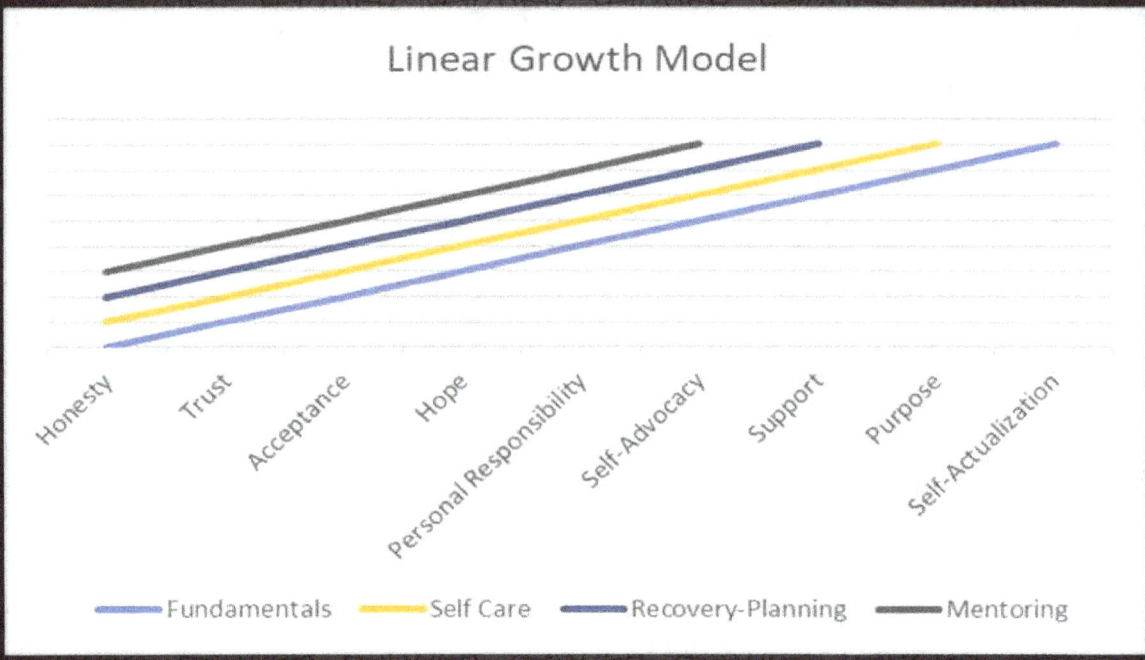

The Linear Growth Model (Continued)

The Linear Growth Model gets its name from the idea that

1. Growth is usually Non-Linear

2. We want to put consistent effort into each of the 9 Fundamentals which will result in more, but not all, consistent experiences in our lives.

3. When developed inconsistently with this format, inconsistent and unexpected outcomes may occur.

4. When developed in the order listed previously, each of the 9 Recovery Fundamentals assists in the cultivation and growth of the other Fundamentals.

5. When Utilizing the Parallel Recovery Concepts in conjunction with the Recovery Fundamentals, we can shift our results to a better outcome

The Linear Growth Model (Continued)

With all the twists and turns and ups and downs of recovery, it can be hard to even tell if growth is occurring. By putting the same amount of effort and care into each of the Recovery Fundamentals, we will get more consistent results than if we were to put all our efforts in one Fundamental.

Because our own actions and behaviors change and impact the world around us, it is common that when we start exhibiting a better relationship with the Recovery Fundamentals, we will experience a mirror effect from the world. We may sometimes wonder why it seems we receive exaggerated reactions or displays of the Fundamentals directed back at us from society but can understand that this may be connected to our own inconsistent demonstrations of the Fundamentals.

False Sense of Security

When we experience success at Recovery Concepts or the later Fundamentals, particularly starting with Personal Responsibility through Self-Advocacy, Support, and Purpose, we may be lulled into a false sense of security that we are doing well despite shortfalls related to the earlier Fundamentals.

We encourage that no matter our level of success with later Fundamentals, we take a look at how the earlier fundamentals show up for us. Gaps in our development may lead to blind spots that may damage our recovery.

Why We Present the Recovery Fundamentals and Parallel Recovery Concepts in This Order

There are many reasons that if we do not take proper care of each Recovery Fundamental and Parallel Recovery Concept, we will not unlock the full growth potential of incorporating Recovery Concepts or Fundamentals into our lives.

We give examples of how neglecting components of the Recovery Concepts and Fundamentals leads to a breakdown of the transition to the other components:

Recovery Concepts:

This group process and other methods of Recovery can be hard on us emotionally, mentally, and physically; therefore, it is important that we are kind to ourselves and benefit from this process.

From the very beginning of an attempt to better ourselves, such as participating in this group, it will be important to maintain the Recovery Concepts of Self-Care, Recovery Planning, and Mentorship.

Right from the beginning it is important to:

- Have a self-care plan, acknowledge the difficulty of this process, and create positive experiences to look forward to

- develop a Recovery plan involving the desired outcome and benefit of this process,

- and recognize that our participation in this process can either help or hinder the recovery of other participants.

Recovery Fundamentals:

Honesty: if we are in fear of what someone will find out about our secrets, harm done to others, past crimes, and the things that make us feel guilt, shame, or fear of persecution, we will not know what we can trust others with.

Trust: If we cannot trust ourselves or are not aware of who we can Trust or what systems are working for us and not against us, we will have a hard time finding acceptance of our situation.

Acceptance: If we can't accept our current situation or past experiences and are constantly suffering from them or if someone or some force has an uncomfortable level of control over our lives, we will have a hard time recognizing things we can hope for.

Recovery Fundamentals:

Hope: If we don't have any hope and are not propelled by our desire to achieve a hoped-for outcome, the natural inclination is to be unmotivated about our personal responsibilities. If we can't get satisfaction by working on our hopes, we often fail to develop and perform personal responsibilities.

Personal Responsibilities: if we are lacking in fulfilling our personal responsibilities, we often face resistance from others when we self-advocate for ourselves because we have less basis to show that we are capable.

Self-Advocacy: If we fail to effectively advocate for ourselves through means of showing that our capabilities or progress make us a good fit for certain endeavors, or if we advocate for ourselves for that which provides outcomes inconsistent with our recovery, or if we advocate to the wrong people, among other things, we may not get adequate support.

Recovery Fundamentals:

Support: A Significant outcome of working through the Recovery Fundamentals leading up to support, is that we find ourselves in the best position to begin offering support.

It takes support to fulfil BIG goals. If we do not look for support or accept support from the right people, we may have a hard time achieving our goals. With the added effort it takes to achieve goals without support, we have a hard time finding our purpose because of the effort and struggle. Often, things that seem more natural or easier for us, or areas where we get the most support, are also the area's excellent to find purpose.

Recovery Fundamentals:

Purpose: Without a purpose with which to gauge our progress or put our efforts, we often feel like we are repeating a pattern that rarely changes, or that there is no perceivable pattern but rather instability or lack of focus. Finding and incorporating a purpose into our lives leads to self-actualization, a feeling that we are fulfilling our unique potential.

Self-Actualization: This Recovery Fundamental is often considered a final stage of development. However, to maintain this stage we must continue to put sufficient and equal amounts of effort into each of the Recovery Fundamentals. Also, a benefit can be found in incorporating the Parallel Recovery Concepts.

Stages of Wellness and Recovery:

Stage one
1 - Learning about recovery
2 - Exercising choice
3 - Seeking services i.e. counseling, therapy, medication, detox, peer support
4 - Staying away from harmful behaviors
5 - Staying away from negative influences, places or people
6 - Ending the pattern of isolation
7 - Finding positive role models
8 - Learning to ask for support
9 - Becoming personally responsible
10 - Experiencing joy and distress that can be overwhelming at times (extreme but fickle)

Stage 2
1 - Increase in physical health
2 - Ability to distinguish between different feelings and handle them
3 - Reducing emotions that interfere with our wellbeing
4 - Changes in thoughts, feelings and beliefs
5 - Zoning in on negative behaviors
6 - Having experienced the benefits of recovery, becoming committed to recovery

Stage 3
1 - Desire to make amends for harm we caused before we began recovery
2 - Becoming the "change we want to see in the world"
3 - Learning not to inflict self-harm or create hardship
4 - Developing honest and trusting relationships with more people

Stage 4
1 - Ability to use our strengths & knowledge to seize opportunities
2 - Automatic use of wellness tools and coping skills
3 - Self-forgiveness
4 - Building loving relationships rather than dependent ones
5 - Experiencing enduring happiness

Stage 5
1 - Becoming Self-actualized
2 - Gaining confidence, gratitude, and acceptance
3 - Developing integrity and humility
4 - Significant reduction of fear

Stage 6 - Celebration & Maintenance

The Guiding Principles of Recovery
Taken from SAMHSA

Hope – belief that recovery is possible. When Hope is internalized and promoted by others, it is a key driver of recovery.

Person-driven – People define their own goals and the path to reaching them.

Many Pathways/Roads – Recovery is highly personalized and different for each person.

Holistic – Recovery emphasizes mind, body, spirit, and community.

Peer Support – Peers encourage and engage each other.

Relational – Recovery is supported by people who believe in a person's ability to recover.

Culture – Traditions, beliefs, and values are important in defining a person's recovery journey and path.

Trauma-Informed – Services should promote safety and trust, creating choice, empowerment, and collaboration.

Strengths & Responsibilities – Individuals, communities, and families have strengths and resources that can benefit recovery. Individuals have the responsibility for their own recovery, but family and community support is essential.

Respect – acceptance and appreciation is key to recovery. This includes respect from other people and a respect for ourselves that helps us develop a positive identity and confidence.

What Mentors should know

- Peer Support is **Self-directed** and works on the principle that clients are the experts on their own experiences and needs. It is a type of therapy based on the idea that each person can become more self-aware, take charge of their own lives, and improve. It is **Person-driven** – People define their own goals and the path to reaching them.

- Peer Support uses **Empathy** a key component of emotional intelligence. **Empathy** is the ability to understand and accurately perceive the internal experiences of another person. In client-centered counseling, Supporters try to show empathy by actively listening to clients, considering their feelings and experiences, and communicating and accepting them.

- In Peer Support, **empowerment** can come from facilitating self discovery and growth by allowing people to to make their own choices and decisions based on their own values, priorities, and goals. The therapist supports the client in identifying their strengths, resources, and areas for growth and assists them in developing coping strategies, problem-solving skills, and self-care practices. **Empathy** also helps counteract **learned helplessness** by creating a safe and supportive environment where clients feel **empowered** to take ownership of their lives and make positive changes.

What Mentors should know

- The **Trauma Informed Approach** demands trust and safety at all levels. This practice encourages choice, collaboration, and empowerment. To practice the Trauma informed approach, request and accommodate feedback as to how to increase the safety of the environment, increase trust by practicing genuineness, and create choice by using open ended and permission questions.

- **Stages of Change** – Stages of change include **Precontemplation, Contemplation, Preparation, Action, and Maintenance**. Often mentors will fail helping someone change behaviors because they do not approach change in the order previously listed. In Precontemplation we educate and develop discrepancy, in Contemplation we encourage and view pros and cons, in Preparation we dismantle barriers, in Action we validate, in Maintenance we should encourage consistency and acquiring more skills related to successful outcomes related to the goal or behavior.

- Some **Cognitive Behavioral Therapy (CBT)** is outside the scope of a Peer Recovery Supporter. Various practices like desensitization techniques and use of imagery are concepts best left to qualified clinicians. However, **relaxation therapy** may be utilized as well as **cognitive behavioral workbooks** that are crafted to address **thoughts, beliefs, and feelings** in a way that does not create excessive pressure on the mentee. Person centered techniques such as building trust and rapport are often helpful but not required as some mentees prefer a more distant expert approach, however this too is outside the scope of a Peer Recovery Supporter.

Differentiate between the medical model and the wellness-focused approach to recovery.

The Medical Model is primarily related to Psychiatry. In the medical model, expert Psychiatrists consider the problems being experienced to be related to genetic inheritance or chemical imbalances. They rely on Medication Assisted Therapy to cause positive change in their patients. This is different from the approach of a Social Worker, Therapist, or Peer Supporter.

A Wellness-focused Approach often involves Peer Support, or the support of someone with lived experience of mental health or substance use; moreover, it considers Social Determinants of Health such as housing, employment, and social support as significant factors of wellbeing.

A Wellness-focused Approach involves **growth, meaning, purpose,** and **empowerment** beyond the problem, which helps a person live the life they want to live.

Day 2

Make sure to prepare for the special exercise found in the section for Self-Care.

Self-Care requires us to make a list of 5 wellness activities we can use to help ourselves feel better. We will discuss our lists of wellness activities in group or in breakout rooms. Please be prepared ahead of time.

Please complete responses to passages and questions included in future groups such as "Day 2" before the next group.

Instructions for passage responses – 1) response must include 5 keywords found in the passage itself. 2) Ensure that the keywords get <u>underlined</u>, so we know which ones you used. 3) the Recovery Concept or Fundamental being linked to the passage must be mentioned <u>twice</u> in the response.

NOTES:

Radical Recovery
Peer Support – Day 2

Insights on Self-Care

Self-care is any healthy action we take to feel better. Sometimes we use Self-Care to respond to stressors, triggering events, or when we feel like we are in crisis. Self-Care that might work normally may not work as well under very difficult conditions.

Tip for dealing with stressors: One suggestion for how to deal with especially difficult situations is to put more time and effort into the things we usually do to make us feel better.

Really good Self-Care is often planned. Planning Self-Care before we feel unwell has benefits, such as, having something to look forward to or helping us not forget Self-Care. Because of this, it is often included in recovery planning.

Examples of Self-Care

- Remembering our boundaries and what we will or will not do
- Being of service to others
- Writing a gratitude list
- Spending time with family and friends
- Getting enough sleep
- Taking breaks

Stressors, burnout, vicarious trauma, poor time management, and compassion fatigue are common reasons we provide Self-Care for ourselves.

Doing Something Nice for Yourself- (Page 64) Better Days – A Mental Health Recovery Workbook

For those of us who live with mental health struggles, our lives can often feel overwhelmed by adversity. When we are going through our recovery process, we can be so focused on taking care of all the aspects of our lives that we want or need to improve, that we often skip enjoying simple pleasures such as sitting in the sun reading a good book, going to the movies, going on a picnic, or playing with a puppy. For all the hard work we do to nurture our recovery process we also deserve to laugh and smile because it is so good for our mind body and soul.

As individuals with mental health struggles our lives are often very complicated. We are worthy of doing nice things for ourselves, especially while dealing with lives complicated by triggers and frustrations. If we can take some time to do something nice for ourselves, the result is that Better Days are on the way and Better Days are here to stay.

- The assignment "how does this passage relate to...?" must include 5 keywords from the passage itself which cannot be used or counted more than once. In addition, the Recovery Concept or Fundamental must be mentioned at least twice in the assignment. <u>Words that do not convey a concept like we, the, or, or a, will not be counted.</u>
- Variations of words that are <u>used in the passages</u> are accepted such as changing "Simple" to "Simplest."
- You must underline the keywords you use.

Example - How Does the Passage connect to Self-Care?

The Passage reminds us that while we are <u>focused</u> on our most essential goals and challenges first (I.e., the things we want or need) we may overlook <u>simple pleasures</u> that can give us joy with little effort. Actively participating in things that bring us joy is an example of <u>Self-Care</u>. The simplest of actions/pleasures is often the most accessible option.

Because we often are playing catch up rather than being ahead of the curve and because we are weighed down by stressors, <u>triggers</u>, and things that make life <u>complicated</u>, sometimes we believe we aren't worthy of or don't deserve nice things in our lives. But it is because of these challenges that we must find simple methods of <u>Self-Care</u> by doing <u>nice</u> things for ourselves.

How Does the Passage connect to Self-Care?

HOMEWORK

Question - 1:
What are 3 Simple Pleasures That Make You Happy?

HOMEWORK

1. -

2. -

3. -

Question - 2:
Why is It Important to Be Gentle to Yourself?

HOMEWORK

Question - 3:
How Will Our Lives Improve by Spending Time Enjoying Simple Pleasures

HOMEWORK

Homework – Provide a List of Wellness Activities

1.
2.
3.
4.
5.

NOTES:

Recovery Planning

Recovery planning is self-determined but often includes friends and family, supporters, or community leaders. Recovery planning is done with the collaboration of individuals involved and utilizes recovery capital.

A Recovery Plan

- *Is based on self-determination*

- *Identifies strengths of the individual and takes inventory of Recovery Capital*

- *Identifies goals, challenges, action steps, and date of completion*

- *may involve support from others and connection to community resources and leadership.*

- *need to be evaluated and measured for progress. Criteria for evaluation should come from the person creating the plan and should be considered before action, if possible.*

What a Recovery Plan Looks Like on Paper

Goal	Strengths & Recovery Capital	Challenges	Action Steps	Date of Completion
Get Masters Degree	<ul><li>Have a: bachelors degree</li><li>Time: Am on Disability and am self employed</li><li>Experienced with: online courses</li></ul>	Classes are condensed so more is required in a shorter time.	<ul><li>Clear agenda for first week</li><li>Start each day with school first</li><li>Complete all assignments before recreation</li></ul>	August 10th 2025

Recovery Planning – (Page 32)
Better Days – A Mental Health Recovery Workbook

Struggling is part of recovery; therefore we all experience tough times. If we learn better ways to manage those tough days in which we are triggered and or having difficulties, we will be happier and healthier in the long run.

If we learn better ways to nurture our recovery process we can do better and feel better. We can have more control over how we feel when things are tough.

If we want things to be better, we must make healthy choices to work toward our better day.

I know all of this to be true based on my own personal experiences. The reality is that if we want to feel better then we need to work at it.

When we are struggling, we can work toward making things better, we can choose to help ourselves move through our recovery process.

We will succeed!

How does this Passage Connect With Recovery Planning?

- This passage mentions better ways to handle situations; these <u>better ways</u> are actions we can take to improve our lives. It says that doing this will help us <u>control</u> how we feel when times are tough. A <u>Recovery Plan</u> is a set of actions that we self-select that hold value. When times are tough working on this plan can move us from where we are now to where we want to be.

- The author states their own <u>personal experience</u> and that from it they know work must be done if we want to <u>feel better</u>. From my experience, it is work that comes through my <u>Recovery Plan</u> that has the most impact on how I feel.

How does this Passage Connect With Recovery Planning

HOMEWORK

Question - 1:
Name and Explain One Method That You Currently Use To Get Back On Track During Tough Times

HOMEWORK

Question - 2:
Give an Example of One Way that You Would Like to Learn How to Help Yourself Feel Better

HOMEWORK

Question - 3:
What Does Recovery Mean to You

HOMEWORK

NOTES:

MENTORING

- Mentoring provides an opportunity to be there for a person in a way that supports them in both the best of times and the worst

- A Mentor utilizes self-disclosure in a way that does not compete with but rather informs an individual of shared experiences

- A good mentor will respect each person's unique approach to recovery

- A Mentor should be primarily focused on the person they are mentoring; only sharing about themselves when it would benefit the mentee

- We never know just what kind of impact we will have on others

- Mentoring is constant and ongoing, and occurs in situations where we present the best or worst aspects of ourselves

What Mentors Should Do

- Identify personal issues that negatively impact one's ability to perform mentor duties and perform appropriate self care before assisting others further.
- Utilize consultation regarding dual relationships.
- Utilize de-escalation techniques and educate individuals on suicide prevention concepts.
- Partner with the individual to access recovery-oriented services and supports
- Support the individual to identify options and participate in decisions connected to creating and completing recovery goals.
- Promote a wellness-focused approach to recovery.
- Utilize supervision and consultation regarding harm to self and others.
- Respond appropriately to personal stressors, triggers and indicators.
- Utilize trauma-informed care approaches.
- Assess the mentee's satisfaction with his/her progress toward recovery goals.

What Mentors Should Do

- Participate as a member of the individual's treatment team.
- Guarantee that recovery is based on the individual's strengths and resiliencies.
- Support the individual in defining spirituality on their own terms.
- Assist others to develop problem-solving skills.
- Assure that relationships, services and supports, reflect individual differences and cultural diversity.
- Support the individual's use of self-determination.
- Model acceptance and cultural humility.
- Partner with individuals to assist them in identifying their strengths, challenges to recovery and recovery capital.
- Apply Motivational Interviewing to assist individuals in during stages of change.
- Inform individuals of their options related to decisions that affect their recovery.

Mahatma Gandhi

- Remember the words of Mahatma Gandhi – **"be the change you want to see in the world."**
- One way to effect change is through Mentoring.

Sometimes We Struggle (Page 4)
Better Days – A Mental Health Recovery Workbook

There are days when I feel so bad that I become unable to see things for how they really are. Often my thoughts are twisting and turning throughout a maze of total and brutal negativity I find myself gasping for air and grasping for a hand to hold onto, yet sometimes it seems that I am very alone.

I ask myself - is this struggle for Wellness and recovery worthy of all my efforts? Why am I dedicating all my hard work and time and effort toward my recovery? What is this recovery that I am fighting so hard for?

It is important for us to think of the big picture. When we Work hard to improve our quality of life and strengthen our coping skills, we will experience beneficial results. When we struggle, experience difficulties in question or recovery, we can and will take back our lives and celebrate our progress and accept that sometimes, we all struggle.

Our struggle has meaning and our recovery is here to stay.

How does this Passage Connect With Mentoring?

HOMEWORK

Question – 1:
Do You Believe There is Meaning and Value in Your Struggle and Why?

HOMEWORK

Question – 2:
In Your Daily Life, How Do You Manage the Ups and Downs That You Face Without Being Thrown Off Course?

HOMEWORK

Question – 3:
What are Three Reasons You Are Fighting for Your Recovery?

HOMEWORK

1:

2:

3:

Creating Change - (Page 16)
Better Days – A Mental Health Recovery Workbook

People say that change comes from within. This saying applies to most people, including people living with mental health struggles.

What does it mean to change from within?

When I have something about myself or my life that I want to improve, I must work hard and implement changes in how I do things. I achieve this by focusing my thoughts on my goals and by taking healthy actions for change.

Mahatma Gandhi, the great Indian spiritual leader, said, "be the change you want to see in the world" I say that first I must change myself into the person I want to be.

The ability to choose to change ourselves for the better is something that no one can take away from us. We can and will live better lives, beginning with having a better day starting today.

How does this Passage Connect With Mentoring?

HOMEWORK

Question – 1:
What are the Top 3 Things That You Want To Change About Yourself?

HOMEWORK

1:

2:

3:

Question – 2:
What Good Things Have You Gained From Your Struggle With Mental Wellbeing?

HOMEWORK

Question – 3:
What is the Number One Thing You Can Do Today To Improve Your Life for the Better?

HOMEWORK

Being in the Moment – (Page 40)
Better Days – A Mental Health Recovery Workbook

In the past week, my recovery experience has taught me so much. My inner pain is erupting like a volcano and damaging all in my path. This cycle plagues me time and time again and derails my recovery.

No more will I allow myself to give in to the pain and extreme negativity that I feel at times. Never again will I allow myself to suffer without also trying to fight my way out of my pain. I can and I will learn better ways to manage my life when I am struggling.

WE WILL allow our recovery to heal us and we will grow and live a better quality of life. When we struggle, we decide in that moment if we want to make things better. If we want better days we must work hard to have them.

How does this Passage Connect With Mentoring?

HOMEWORK

Question – 1:
What Does "Being in the Moment" Mean to You?

HOMEWORK

Question – 2:
What Are Three Things That You Can Do When You Are Struggling So You Can Start To Feel Better?

HOMEWORK

1:

2:

3:

Question – 3:
Do You Believe That it Is Possible to Learn Better Ways to Manage Your Life?

HOMEWORK

Working Through Pain – (Page 58)
Better Days – A Mental Health Recovery Workbook

I've been suffering in pain for nearly two weeks. I keep getting better and then getting worse again. I've had to force myself to go to school, and be active and social, and follow through with my general daily responsibilities and activities. I know I am not the only person who knows what suffering feels like. I know that there are others like me who can understand and who have empathy for me.

How do we get ourselves to eat, sleep, bathe, talk, laugh, love, find peace, find happiness and find our recovery process when it feels lost? How do we find our better day - how do we keep moving forward in life when we feel broken or stuck?

How does this Passage Connect With Mentoring?

HOMEWORK

Question – 1:

I Ask My Loved Ones and My Supporters to Remind Me That My Pain "Will Pass" When I am Suffering. In What Ways Can People Support You to Help You When You Are Suffering?

HOMEWORK

Question – 2:

When Your Feeling Overwhelmed, What Are Two Healthy Things That You Can Do to Help Yourself Feel Better?

HOMEWORK

1:

2:

Question – 3:
What is One Thing That You Have Done This Week That You Struggled with Yet Succeeded at Accomplishing?

HOMEWORK

When Good Things Happen – (Page 24)
The Original Peer Support Recovery & Coping Skills Workbook & Curriculum

I can't believe it.

I have experienced so much pain, hurt and difficulty in my life that I sometimes become unable to accept good things when they happen.

This is an honest reaction to a very tough life.

I have put in a lot of hard work to make improvements in my life and to be in recovery.

Recovery is a constant daily process that we must always put our effort toward in order to live the better life we want and to have better days.

Today, thankfully, several good things happened.

It was unexpected. However, these good things are a testament to all of my effort, hard work and dedication that I have put toward my recovery and living a better life.

Sometimes good things happen, and we need to accept, acknowledge, and celebrate these good things.

Why, you ask? Because we are worth it!

How does this Passage Connect With Mentoring?

HOMEWORK

Question – 1:
The Best Part of Being in Recovery Is

HOMEWORK

Question – 2:
The Most Difficult Part of Being in Recovery Is

HOMEWORK

Question – 3:
When I Am Upset; the Best Thing I Can do to Take Care of Myself Is

HOMEWORK

Positive Risk – (Page 20)
The Original Peer Support Recovery & Coping Skills Workbook & Curriculum

This weekend, I took a step forward in my recovery. I took a positive risk. I was scared and nervous, however, I stood up to my feelings and I succeeded.

It is never easy having to take a chance. Recovery is such a precious thing. I know that in order to live a better quality life, I must take some chances. I am talking about taking a positive risk. This is how I move forward.

I must give myself the chance to heal; to get better.

No one will do it for me; only I can do it for myself.

Sometimes we have to invest in our better future, better day by better day by better day.

How does this Passage Connect With Mentoring?

HOMEWORK

Question – 1:
What do you do to move forward after something intense and upsetting happens in your life?

HOMEWORK

Question – 2:
What is a positive risk that you have taken recently?

HOMEWORK

Question – 3:
What is one thing you would like to improve about your life and how you live it?

HOMEWORK

The Homework – In the next Year I will

For the current year;

- Create a Recovery Plan Involving 7 goals/activities that you have every day and some activities you will need to do every once in awhile. In the area for the date, if it is not ongoing, list the date of completion; if it is ongoing, state whether it is something that is done every day, or how often it will be done. Please include **both** <u>daily tasks</u> and <u>those we must do every now and then</u>.

- Start with things you struggle with rather than things you find easy.

- Next, create a list of 7 big goals you have, or things that are vitally important that you want to or must do within the year.

- Ensure that this list/Recovery Plan includes how you will support your basic needs like shelter, food and bills. Make the goal specific and attainable.

- During Day 4 we will present a goal from each category of the Recovery Plan and the action steps for the goal.

NOTES:

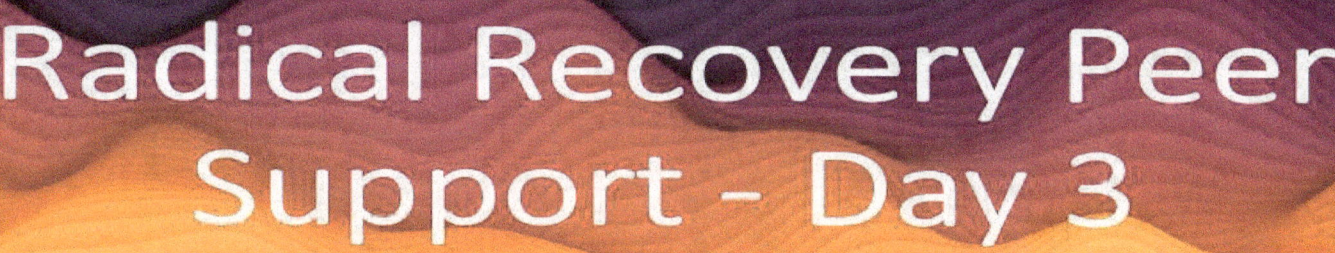

Honesty

Many of us have Baggage. In recovery, we may resist new healthy behaviors and thoughts. This may often stem from a lack of honesty about three factors, 1: that we have been hurt, 2: that we have hurt ourselves or others, and 3: the nature of the severity of the hurt.

It is important to acknowledge

- if we are not honest with ourselves about how we have been hurt, hurt ourselves or others, or the severity, we may repeat unfavorable experiences.

- **Lets take a minute to be honest with ourselves about ourselves. On page 152 and 153 you will find a list of virtues, values, and character defects. Please read the directions and complete the activity. Every person has some of each, please indicate at least <u>five</u> of each.**

Accountability (Page 6)
Better Days: A Mental Health Recovery Workbook

I have made countless mistakes over the course of my life. I have damaged others and I have damaged myself.

It is said that time heals all wounds. What does this mean? Is this true?

I think that taking responsibility for our actions can be an empowering process. Each of us possesses the ability to liberate ourselves from the chains of our past. The decisions that we make today and tomorrow are a gateway toward a Better Day in a better life.

How Does the Passage Connect to Honesty?

HOMEWORK

HOMEWORK

Question - 1:
List three ways that your life has been affected by decisions that you have made

1. -

2. -

3. -

HOMEWORK

Question - 2:
Name one mistake that you have made in your life and what you learned because of it

HOMEWORK

Question - 3:
List three things that you want to improve in your life and what you can do to make them happen

1. -

2. -

3. -

Being Self Aware (Page – 10)
Better Days: A Mental Health Recovery Workbook

One of the most important components of mental health recovery is being self-aware.

What does it mean to be self-aware?

Are you aware of how you speak to people?

Are you aware of how others perceive you when you are communicating with them?

Are you aware of your body language and the message your body language sends to others?

Are you aware of your attitude?

Are you aware of how you are improving your life?

Are you aware of the things that you do that are causing you problems?

Can being self-aware help you to get to where you want to go in life?

How Does the Passage Connect to Honesty?

HOMEWORK

Question - 1:
In what two ways are you self-aware?

HOMEWORK

1. -

2. -

Question - 2:
What are two things that you know about yourself that you would like to change or improve?

HOMEWORK

1. -

2. -

Question - 3:
How can being more self-aware make your life better?

HOMEWORK

NOTES:

Trust

There are different levels of trust:

We can have trust in

- a specific person or people that we trust
- in the systems we are in, such as our governments, legal system, or system of wellness or therapy
- self-trust; <u>trusting that we have our own best interests in mind.</u>

Within these is determining who we can rely on, who we cannot, and what we can share with others.

Tip – (Trust)

- ❖ **Self-disclosure: It is important to remember**
    - we never need to share something that would make us uncomfortable
    - there is more we can share with others than something that would make us uncomfortable
    - it is different to share things we want to keep private versus our hopes, goals, and stresses
    - there is no guarantee what we say will remain confidential

Dealing With Conflict: Trusting Others (Page 34)
Original Peer Support Recovery & Coping Skills Workbook and Curriculum

In my life, I have experienced a great deal of conflict. At times, I have struggled with knowing which people I can get the most helpful support from. This is an issue of trust. Let's talk about what trust is and how having a trustworthy confidant is important to your recovery: Having a safe person who you can trust to help you is important. Having that person will help you feel less alone in your struggle.

As people in recovery, our lives present countless opportunities for us to develop trust in others and to learn to trust in ourselves. We can create better days, one trusting moment at a time because we do not need to be alone in our struggle.

How Does the Passage Connect to Trust?

HOMEWORK

Question - 1:
List the names of three people who you can trust if you are having an intense challenge

HOMEWORK

1. -

2. -

3. -

HOMEWORK

Question - 2:
How do you manage a tough situation when you don't have someone to talk to for support?

HOMEWORK

Question - 3:
Why is being able to trust others important to your recovery?

The Importance of Companionship (Page 46)
Better Days: A Mental Health Recovery Workbook

As a person who lives with a mental health struggle, I am well aware of how lonely and alone my life can feel at times. I have learned that it is possible to make progress toward improving my relationships. However, this requires hard work.

Why is companionship so important for a person going through the recovery process?

Do you feel that you can count on your peers to be supportive and listen if you need them to? Let's think about our lives - are there people in yours that you can reach out to? Perhaps offer support to each other? Perhaps build friendships with?

As people living with a mental health struggle, our lives can feel very alone. We can change this for the better and find happiness, companionship and peace.

How Does the Passage Connect to Trust?

HOMEWORK

HOMEWORK

Question - 1:
Name one worthwhile friendship that you have in your life.
What are the best parts about having this friendship?

HOMEWORK

Question - 2:
What does having a good friend mean to you?
What does it mean to be a good friend?

Question - 3:
Why is peer support and friendship so important to have when a person is in the recovery process?

HOMEWORK

The Value in Our Struggle
Better Days: A Mental Health Recovery Workbook

I sit here very tired, sick and cold and feeling useless. It is as if my body continues to struggle towards mental Wellness independently of my conscious mind. I think this is because somewhere along my journey to recovery I found hope and promise and options in my struggle. The struggle has never been easy for me. It has been a constant life lesson knocking me down and then helping me up over and over again.

Our struggles have value. The struggles of every person using this workbook are valuable. Our struggles teach us how to live and how to be. Someday we will look back and say thank goodness for the experiences we have had and for how much we have grown, and then we will realize that we are strong, and we can be proud, and we can celebrate our lives.

How Does the Passage Connect to Trust?

HOMEWORK

Question - 1:
When you feel terrible, unable to function or manage your life, what are two things that you can do to get yourself back on track?

1. -

2. -

HOMEWORK

Question - 2:
What are two things that you can ask someone else to help you with during you times of need?

HOMEWORK

1. -

2. -

Question - 3:
Looking back over your life, what are two experiences in which you have struggled and then found that you had learned a good and helpful lesson?

HOMEWORK

1. -

2. -

Acceptance

Each person is subject to different degrees of unforeseen circumstances, restrictions, rules, and regulations. For the most part, these obstacles depend on our situation, can be temporary, or can be changed with support. While we must deal with these situations while they occur, we can find ways to have hope within them and have Better Days.

*Tip – Trauma/Grief Informed: Many people will report that there are things that they cannot or will not accept. This is okay, remind them that they can still work on other Fundamentals and that there is a difference between 1: accepting that an event took place and 2: accepting an event into our lives and our space.

WE MUST KEEP MOVING

Sometimes, it is the things we find the hardest to accept that take us off the path of our life purpose.

Dr. Martin Luther King Jr. believed that the most important thing each person must do is figure out their life purpose and let nothing hold them back from being the very best at the purpose they have chosen.

While we may struggle to find acceptance, we can let nothing hold us back; in the words of Dr. King **"We must keep moving. If you can't fly, run; if you can't run, walk; if you can't walk, crawl; but by all means keep moving."**

We Cant Control Everything – (Page 38)
Better Days: A Mental Health Recovery Workbook

The recovery journey can introduce many wonderful experiences into our lives. with that said there are things that may happen in our daily life that are completely out of our control.

In my experience, I have found that part of living in this world is having to face the fact that I am unable to control all the parts of my life.

Yesterday, I had to face being insulted and have some very hurtful things said to me about me for something that was not my responsibility in any way. I had no control over the cause of this situation. However as I was a bearer of some bad news, I became the target.

I hurt. And I hurt a lot.

Then my day went on and my life went on, and it was up to me to accept there are things that I cannot control, that I have done my very best and that, unfortunately, things don't always workout the way I would like them to; however, my life does go on and I will continue to work as hard as humanly possible to achieve my Better Days.

How Does the Passage Connect to Acceptance?

HOMEWORK

Question - 1:
Take five minutes and ask a safe person to talk with you about any topic that you are interested in that is unrelated to your struggle. How did things go for you?

HOMEWORK

Question - 2:
Then take five minutes and ask that same person how they are doing today. Then ask that person to ask you how you are doing. This is Peer Support.

HOMEWORK

Question - 3:
When things happen that are out of your control, what are three things that you can do to help yourself feel better and to have a Better Day?

HOMEWORK

1. -

2. -

3. -

Experiencing Recovery – (Page 40)
Original Peer Support Recovery & Coping Skills Workbook and Curriculum

Today may be the beginning of my being well. I must be realistic; it is absolutely possible that I might be feeling better as of today.

Things in my life could be a lot worse. I have suffered and my suffering has been a great teacher. If there is a lesson out there to be taught, I want to learn it. I suspect that I may have been well these past several weeks and just not have known it.

Perhaps this was a necessary part of experiencing recovery. If I am hurting yet stay on track, that is recovery. If you are struggling or in despair and you continue to work hard to keep yourself together, this is recovery.

How Does the Passage Connect to Acceptance?

HOMEWORK

Question - 1:
What Does it Mean to you to experience recovery?

HOMEWORK

Question - 2:
In what ways do you know that you are doing well?

HOMEWORK

Question - 3:
How does this coping skills guide help you improve the quality of your life?

HOMEWORK

Accepting Your Life – (Page 42)
Original Peer Support Recovery & Coping Skills Workbook and Curriculum

Life happens.

Life will go on whether things have been fair or not.

Life will go on if you have made a big mistake.

Life will go on if you win $1,000,000.

Life will go on no matter what.

Life will go on if you break your arm.

Life will go on if you have surgery.

Life will go on if you have a financial crisis.

Life will go on. Your life will continue.

Accepting Your Life (Continued)

We must accept that life will happen and sometimes there is nothing that we can do about it. If we suffer pain, loneliness, regret, embarrassment or any other difficult feeling, we must accept our life. We must accept our life and we must accept our reality. We must also accept that each and everyone of us has the power within to make a Better Day for ourselves no matter what the circumstances we find ourselves in.

Life will go on no matter what.

I know that I will live my life fighting for that Better Day because I have to.

I have no other option. Better Days are on the way and Better Days are here to stay.

How Does the Passage Connect to Acceptance?

HOMEWORK

Question - 1:
What are three things that you feel are unfair about your life?

HOMEWORK

1. -

2. -

3. -

Question - 2:
In what three ways do you live your life in a hopeful way?

HOMEWORK

1. -

2. -

3. -

Question - 3:
What are three steps that you could take to make your life better today?

HOMEWORK

1. -

2. -

3. -

Day 4 - Introduction

Please be prepared to discuss a goal for each category of your 1-year Recovery Plan.

Have a great week!

NOTES:

Hope

If we are struggling to find hope, it will often become easier the longer we commit to recovery and with more time between distressing events. Also, we can seek out inspiration by:

- talking to supporters about what is giving our supporters hope
- making lists of things that give us hope
- reading recovery stories
- listing our dreams, and if possible, communicating them to someone

Hope – (Page 4)
Original Peer Support Recovery & Coping Skills Workbook & Curriculum

On Somedays, hope is all I have.

I will fight to live a better life because I want to be happy and successful and because I deserve it.

No one else can tell me that I can't have a better life in which I am happy and healthy.

We decide if we want to live a good and healthy life.

We must reject negative and unhelpful thinking.

Each of us has the power within us to change for the better.

Each of us has a responsibility to work as hard as we can to improve our lives.

We are in control of our lives. Allow yourself to be in control of your life.

We will rise above stigma and be all that we can be.

It will be your victory.

How Does the Passage Connect to Hope?

HOMEWORK

Question - 1:
What are five things that I am proud of in my life?

HOMEWORK

HOMEWORK

Question - 2:
What are five things that I most want to improve in my life?

HOMEWORK

Question - 3: Recovery is -?

Inspiration - (Page 36)
Original Peer Support Recovery & Coping Skills Workbook & Curriculum

What is inspiration? What does it mean to be inspired?

As a person who is a peer supporter I come in contact with many people who may be struggling yet want to make things better.

These individuals might benefit from some words of encouragement or an expression of mutual support and understanding.

The people I find inspiring are the ones who are trying hard to improve their lives.

These people make me want to develop and facilitate the Better Days group every week.

Inspiration – (Continued)

This is because I feel inspired by being part of this group.

I want to work hard to improve my life.

Sharing with others who are also trying to make their lives better is inspiring.

Finding your inspiration is a vital component to recovery and Wellness.

When we are able to recognize what it is that inspires us to live better lives, we then are better able to live those lives.

How Does the Passage Connect to Hope?

HOMEWORK

Question - 1:
List three things in your life that inspire you

HOMEWORK

Question - 2:
Give an example of when you think that you inspired another person

HOMEWORK

Question - 3:
This workbook inspires me to

HOMEWORK

Pain Will Pass
Original Peer Support Recovery & Coping Skills Workbook & Curriculum

On some days, I feel as if I am carrying a 1000 pound weight on my back. On some days, I feel depression, fear, loneliness, grief, and helplessness.

I acknowledge that I do not always know what to do when it comes to dealing with the intensities that I face, sometimes daily, in my life.

One thing that I do know is that the pain and hurt will pass. The pain and hurt that often feels so overwhelming; it will pass, and I will grow from my experiences.

We will learn better ways to have Better Days regardless of how much we may struggle from one day to the next.

How Does the Passage Connect to Hope?

HOMEWORK

HOMEWORK

Question - 1:
What are three positive things that we can learn from our experiences with experiencing emotional pain?

HOMEWORK

Question - 2:
When you feel overwhelmed, in what ways do you seek help (who do you call, ask for support, etc.)?

Question - 3:

What is one new thing that might help you consider trying to cope with and heal from the pain you experience?

HOMEWORK

NOTES:

Personal Responsibility

Some situations may be out of our control or cause discomfort for us. If we are having a hard time fulfilling responsibilities because of obstacles, things outside our control, or things we need or are worried about; we can ask how much control we have over these situations, and if we are doing everything we can within the control we have.

To get back on track we can follow a Recovery Plan that involves:

- A daily plan
- A plan of things we need to do every now and then
- A plan for achieving big goals

Plans should include a way to provide for ourselves and elements of Self-Care.

Personal Responsibility (Continued)

If we are developing a Recovery Plan, it is important to first list things we struggle with, things that need the most attention, or that create new responsibilities for us.

A Recovery Plan is a way to familiarize ourselves with our objectives and requirements and decide how things need to be done.

Personal Responsibility may involve creating goals that improve our lives and our success. For information on how to help someone with their goals, refer to the section of the RRPS Recovery & Mentorship Guide titled Motivational Interviewing & Recovery Planning.

Getting Back on Track - (Page 30)
Original Peer Support Recovery & Coping Skills Workbook & Curriculum

The past few weeks have been very difficult for me.

I have not been doing well.

I know what it is that triggered me.

There is very little that I can do about it. What I can do is take steps to improve myself, work on strengthening my coping skills and move forward.

One thing that I can do is focus on getting myself back on track toward being healthy and happy.

I have suffered enough, and I want my life back.

I choose how I react to things in my life, and I decide if I want to move forward.

I can take positive steps to feel emotional and mental relief and I can, and I will succeed at this.

I will work hard for my better days, and I will achieve my goals.

We can all take steps toward achieving our goals!

It will be your victory!

How Does the Passage Connect to Personal Responsibility?

HOMEWORK

Question - 1:
List three things that you can do to get back on track when you're struggling.

HOMEWORK

1:

2:

3:

Question - 2:

Name one thing that you struggle with and two ways in which you can effectively deal with it.

HOMEWORK

Question - 3:

In your opinion is it possible to gain more control over how we react to the difficult things that we face in our lives?

HOMEWORK

Staying Strong- (Page 35)
Better Days- A Mental Health Recovery Workbook

When we have a tough day, it can be hard to follow through with all of our responsibilities. On these tough days, we must ask ourselves that if we are not feeling 100%, are we still able to successfully go to our appointments, work, school, social commitments, etc.?

Sometimes we need to accept that we have it within ourselves to battle though our difficulties and continue to move forward toward our goals.

In my experience it is absolutely possible to work through difficulty and find wellness and success. Yesterday was a tough day for me, yet I stayed strong and worked hard and it ended up being an incredibly wonderful day.

How Does the Passage Connect to Personal Responsibility?

HOMEWORK

Question - 1:

What are three situations that you might choose where it would be better to stay at home when you are not feeling 100%?

HOMEWORK

1:

2:

3:

Question - 2:

What are three situations that you might choose to battle through and move forward with your day, even if you are not feeling 100%?

HOMEWORK

1:

2:

3:

Question - 3:

Name two situations in which you stuck with your plan and responsibilities for the day and then realized you were feeling better. Why do you think you were feeling better?

HOMEWORK

1.

2.

Working Through Pain – (Page 58)
Better Days – A Mental Health Recovery Workbook

I've been suffering in pain for nearly two weeks. I keep getting better and then getting worse again. I've had to force myself to go to school, and be active and social, and follow through with my general daily responsibilities and activities. I know I am not the only person who knows what does suffering feels like. I know that there are others like me who can understand and who have empathy for me.

How do we get ourselves to eat, sleep, bathe, talk, laugh, love, find peace, find happiness and find our recovery process when it feels lost? How do we find our better day how do we keep moving forward in life when we feel broken or stuck?

How Does the Passage Connect to Personal Responsibility?

HOMEWORK

Question – 1:
I Ask My Loved Ones and My Supporters to Remind Me That My Pain "Will Pass" When I am Suffering. In What Ways Can People Support You to Help You When You Are Suffering?

HOMEWORK

Question – 2:
When Your Feeling Overwhelmed, What Are Two Healthy Things That You Can Do to Help Yourself Feel Better?

HOMEWORK

Question – 3:
What is One Thing That You Have Done This Week That You Struggled with Yet Succeeded at Accomplishing?

HOMEWORK

Choosing Better Ways to React – (Page 72)
Better Days- A Mental Health Recovery Workbook

When we are having a rough day, how can we get through our day successfully and make it better? All people have a bad day once in awhile, and we can choose to make our "bad day" a Better Day.

We can choose how to react to things that happen in our lives, and we can learn to improve our ability to handle things that happen that we don't like. If we can take more responsibility in making better choices for ourselves, then we can have more control over the quality of our lives.

How Does the Passage Connect to Personal Responsibility?

HOMEWORK

Question - 1:

Imagine that someone the lives in your household was very loud last night and you were unable to get enough sleep. How would something like this make you feel; how would you react to the noise and disruption of your sleep?

HOMEWORK

Question - 2:

Imagine that someone the lives in your household was very loud last night and you were unable to get enough sleep. Would your reaction to the noise make things better for you or would your reaction make things worse?

HOMEWORK

Question - 3:
Give one example from your life in which you successfully handled a difficult situation.

HOMEWORK

Doing What's Right (Page 6)
Original Peer Support Recovery & Coping Skills Workbook & Curriculum

I am a person who sometimes experiences extreme feelings.

These feelings caused me to feel excellent and sometimes not so good.

I struggle with knowing what to do with my feelings when they feel so strong.

Sometimes I react to things I experience in exaggerated ways.

Often, when I'm feeling intense emotions, this happens.

I must never forget that I am a human being.

My life will continue moving forward even if I overreact at times.

We can learn from this and find some peace in our lives.

How Does the Passage Connect to Personal Responsibility?

HOMEWORK

Question – 1:
List three situations in your life that cause you to experience strong emotions.

HOMEWORK

1:

2:

3:

Question – 2:

Give one example where you did something positive for yourself even though it was hard to do.

HOMEWORK

Question – 3:

List three experiences that make you feel happy.

HOMEWORK

1:

2:

3:

Being Responsible to Yourself – (Page 18)
Original Peer Support Recovery & Coping Skills Workbook & Curriculum

In order to gain and maintain our recovery, we must take responsibility for ourselves, our lives and our actions. What is responsibility and why is being responsible crucial to having our positive mental health?

There have been times where I have made some poor choices in my life. The best thing that I could do is try and learn from my mistakes. If I am able to acknowledge the choices I make can play a role in how well I am doing on any given day, then, I have found a major tool for experiencing lasting Wellness.

No one besides myself can make me change for the better. Our life experiences have taught us some difficult lessons, so let us all learn from these lessons and grow into our happier, healthy and better lives.

Better Days are absolutely on the way, and without a doubt, are here to stay.

How Does the Passage Connect to Personal Responsibility?

HOMEWORK

Question – 1:
List three things in your life that you want to improve.

HOMEWORK

1:

2:

3:

Question – 2:
list the three biggest obstacles that are in the way of you having a happier and healthier life.

HOMEWORK

1:

2:

3:

Question – 3:

If I want to live a happier and healthier life, what are three things I can do today to make this happen?

HOMEWORK

NOTES:

Self-Advocacy

Sometimes people may feel they have lost their right or ability to advocate for themselves, or that they have lost control of their lives. Each person has the right to advocate for themselves for public benefits and treatment common to their society no matter what the state of their lives.

*Tip – if a person is having a hard time gaining support through self-advocacy, communicate that

- our chances of getting support increase the longer we maintain continued effort with the Recovery Fundamentals that precede this step, especially Personal Responsibility.

- we can believe in ourselves and practice advocating by making a list of goals we think will get the most support and advocating for each item on the list.

What Mentors Should Know

- System Level Advocacy – Advocating for changes to rules, policies, or laws that affect how someone lives their lives.
- Self Advocacy – Because very few people will advocate for us, and because recovery is person-driven, self-advocacy, the process of explaining why you deserve or are qualified for something, is the foundation for a strong recovery.
- Shared decision making – This is the process of a supporter and the person being supported collaborating to develop action plans that are agreed to by both partys.
- Person centered language – Instead of saying "he is an addict", say "name* is a person with an addiction. Instead of saying "they are Bipolar", say "name* is a person diagnosed with Bipolar." Instead of saying "they are a patient", say "name* is a person who is receiving services." Instead of saying "Bro", "Dude", or "Man", say "name*."

What Mentors Should Know

Navigating Services - Mentors will regularly require the services of other professionals to provide support and often make recommendations and referrals for other services. A mentor makes meaningful connections with many local services and leaders. Knowing when to say we don't have all the answers is an important characteristic of a mentor. Finding other providers of services who understand the significance of recovery and wellness versus treatment, and the specific needs for people facing specific challenges is encouraged.

Advocating for Recovery-Oriented Systems involves knowing the organization and leaders of the systems in your area on a deep level. We should develop close relationships with people who might provide recovery services to the people we serve. These deep relationships will inform us if the provider has a recovery-oriented mindset for which to advocate. A Recovery Oriented System of Care is a network of community-based services that meet the total needs of the person in recovery or their families. This includes emotional, occupational, educational, financial, spiritual, physical health, social, and environmental needs.

Self-Advocacy – (Page 12)
Original Peer Support Recovery & Coping Skills Workbook & Curriculum

Throughout much of my life, I can remember that I have had many times that I needed someone to help me and speak up on my behalf. I had so many needs that were not addressed. Even to this day, I am aware of the extreme damage that has been done to me after years of not having my needs met. As a teenager growing up in many unnatural situations, no one spoke up and advocated for my personal and intimate needs. I was just another troubled teenager living in a group home.

One thing that I wish I learned as many years ago was the act of self-advocacy. After living through some extremely dreadful and horrendous situations, I have learned how to better advocate for myself. Most everything that I have in my life, I have as a result of my self-advocacy.

When we are able to effectively speak up about our needs, then our lives will be better. Self-advocacy is our tool - Use it!

How Does the Passage Connect to Self-Advocacy?

HOMEWORK

Question – 1:
Give one example of a time in which you advocated for your needs.

HOMEWORK

Question – 2:
What is one example where you did not speak up in order to have your needs met and what would you do differently next time?

HOMEWORK

Question – 3:
What do the words "self-advocacy" mean to you?

HOMEWORK

Getting Our Needs Met - (Page 24)
Better Days- A Mental Health Recovery Workbook

Our lives can often be so difficult. We have to struggle to have a decent quality of life. My basic needs have so often not been met and, no matter how much I asked or begged for help, I felt ignored.

In the past, I have mostly yelled at or screamed at the people who were there to help me and why I yelled and screamed because no one would ever listen to me, it just made things worse. For me this is so frustrating because I am yelling and screaming to get my needs met because I want to be well.

However, if we can develop better ways to communicate what our needs are, then we will have our needs better met.

Recovery begins one Better Day at a time.

How Does the Passage Connect to Self-Advocacy?

HOMEWORK

Question – 1:
What are three basic needs that you need or want to better address?

HOMEWORK

1:

2:

3:

Question – 2:
What are three helpful ways that we can communicate our needs to a doctor, a staff member, a family member, etc.?

HOMEWORK

1:

2:

3:

Question – 3:
What do you consider are effective ways to communicate?

HOMEWORK

Day 5 Introduction

- Please be prepared to share one goal from each category of your 3-year Recovery Plan for the next group.

NOTES:

Day 5

Support

"It takes support to fulfill BIG goals. If we do not look for support or accept support from the right people, we will have a tougher time achieving our goals."

If we lack support, developing a strong support system benefits from:

- being mutually supportive to others
- doing everything within our control to maintain our personal definition of wellness
- becoming active in the community, a support group, school or other area like employment
- having several supporters so someone will always be available, and we do not overburden anyone.

Authentic Support – (Page 32)
Better Days – A Mental Health Recovery Workbook

You know that feeling that we have when we're having a hard time and someone else authentically relates with our struggle? In those moments when you feel all alone yet there's somebody right there in solidarity with you?! Often these are the moments that change our lives for the better forever.

I personally know how difficult it is to face life's challenges alone. Feeling like there's no one you can call for help, that there's no one who you can trust, or that no one understands or supports your goals is a very lonely and scary place to be.

The power of support makes such an impactful difference in so many of our lives. To be able to relate with another person and to feel safe, and understood and listened to; that's worth a lot. Sometimes to get from where we are to where we want to be, we need support and access to resources and opportunities that on our own would be unobtainable.

For many of us, support has saved our lives; always remember what it was like when we didn't have support, and if you are struggling to get to where you want to be, perhaps new relationships with trusted allies could be a solution.

How Does the Passage Connect to Support?

HOMEWORK

Question - 1:
How does it feel to be understood and accepted by others?

HOMEWORK

Question - 2:
Can you recall a situation in which you received support from another person and how did it make you feel?

HOMEWORK

Question - 3:
What does good support look like to you? What is an example of support that you find unhelpful?

HOMEWORK

Purpose

Once we have maintained progress relevant to our interests and security, are more empowered, and have support, we may find that other people are an extension of ourselves or that we have integrated a cause into our lives.

We may also find that
- human rights
- dignity

and
- freedom

become important to us.

Life Blueprint– Purpose
Dr. Martin Luther King Jr.

"You're going to be deciding as the days and the years unfold, what you will do in life, what your life's work will be.

Once you discover what it will be, set out to do it and do it well.

Be a bush if you can't be a tree.

If you can't be a highway, just be a trail.

If you can't be the sun, be a star, for it isn't by size that you win or you fail, be the best of whatever you are."

Meaningful Activities
Better Days- A Mental Health Recovery Workbook

In order to be happy and healthy, there are a few needs I must have met in my life. One of those needs is that I must be doing something that has meaning and purpose.

I come to the Boston Resource Center (a peer-led recovery community) once a week because I have the need to be involved in something helpful and productive. As a human being, I feel that I must contribute something of value to society. One of the best parts of my entire week is sitting with my peers engaging in conversation about improving the quality of our lives.

Having purpose is something that I always lacked in my life. I needed to do something more. It was hard to make it happen. However, I have made great progress and I've only just begun.

How Does the Passage Connect to Purpose?

HOMEWORK

Question – 1:
What are two things that you do in your life that have meaning for you?

HOMEWORK

1:

2:

Question – 2:
What are two meaningful activities that you would like to add to your life in the next two years?

HOMEWORK

1:

2:

Question – 3:
What steps must you take to add more meaningful activities in your life?

HOMEWORK

Our Lives Have Value – (Page 26)
Better Days- A Mental Health Recovery Workbook

As a person living with a mental health struggle, I have felt personally unfulfilled for most of my life. While growing up, I watched a lot of people I knew go to college, have relationships and become successful. At that same time, I was unemployed, uneducated, irresponsible and using drugs.

It wasn't until I was going through the recovery process and improving the quality of my life that I realized how valuable all my experiences have been.

We are all at different places on our recovery journey and our lives have incredible meaning.

Regardless of what society or the system may tell us, we are all valuable and important people deserving of living good quality lives.

How Does the Passage Connect to Purpose?

HOMEWORK

Question – 1:
List two ways that having a mental health struggle impacts your life

HOMEWORK

1:

2:

Question – 2:
List two constructive things that you have learned as a result of living with a mental struggle

HOMEWORK

1:

2:

Question – 3:
Name three parts of your life that have great meaning for you

HOMEWORK

1:

2:

3:

NOTES:

Self-Actualization

Self-actualization is all about reaching the true potential of our unique selves. Once we have reached our full potential, we may find that we are freer and more capable.

People at this level of development may begin to have a deeper connection with where they believe they fit in the universe, existence, in relation to other people, or with their concept of a higher power.

Self-Actualization (continued)

In the Allegory of the Cave from Plato's *The Republic*, the principal character in the story returns to people who were still "disillusioned" to help them find a better way.

For many, there is a natural inclination by this stage of recovery, to show others a brighter future.

The Parallel Recovery Concept of Mentorship has carried many individuals' recoveries to particularly new heights. Consider the shift in growth demonstrated in the Linear Growth Model due to the Recovery Concept of Mentorship.

Living the Life You Want to Live – (Page 48)
Better Days- A Mental Health Recovery Workbook

Before 2006, I had never heard of the concept of recovery. I had no idea that people living with mental health issues could get better and live decent lives. I always had so many dreams, goals and aspirations that, unfortunately, had not become reality. This was and is something that is very frustrating for me, and I would imagine that I am not The only person who can relate to this. In order to lead the life I want to live, I need to consider that my dreams and goals are real possibilities so that I can work toward living a happier life day, by Better Day, by Better Day, by Better Day.

With hard work and dedication, you can lead a happier, healthier and more satisfying life.

How Does the Passage Connect to Self-Actualization?

HOMEWORK

Question – 1:
What are three goals that you have in your life?

HOMEWORK

1:

2:

3:

Question – 2:
Do you believe that you could achieve any of your goals?

HOMEWORK

Question – 3:
What are two steps that you could take to help yourself achieve your goals?

HOMEWORK

1:

2:

NOTES:

Recap & Conclusion

This curriculum emphasizes balanced linear growth through the development of 9 Recovery Fundamentals and three Parallel Recovery Concepts that occur alongside each of the 9 Fundamentals.

 **The goals of this program are based on the Fundamentals of Recovery and the Recovery Concepts and are to teach participants how to:**

 Learn to develop a Recovery Plan to take recovery to greater heights (Recovery Planning)

 Learn the importance of and how to perform Self-Care

 overcome challenges or troubling thoughts, handle stressful or difficult situations, achieve personal growth and wellness, and live a self-directed life

 learn that while participating in recovery we are at every moment a mentor and a model of recovery behavior

The Linear Growth Model

![Linear Growth Model chart showing Fundamentals, Self Care, Recovery-Planning, and Mentoring across Honesty, Trust, Acceptance, Hope, Personal Responsibility, Self-Advocacy, Support, Purpose, Self-Actualization]

The Linear Growth Model gets its name from the idea that

- Growth is usually Non-Linear
- we want to put consistent effort into each of the 9 Fundamentals which will result in more, but not all, consistent experiences in our lives.
- When developed inconsistently with this format, inconsistent and unexpected outcomes may occur.
- When developed in the order listed previously, each of the 9 Recovery Fundamentals assists in the cultivation and growth of the other Fundamentals.
- When Utilizing the Parallel Recovery Concepts in conjunction with the Recovery Fundamentals, we can shift our results to a better outcome

Mahatma Gandhi, the great Indian spiritual leader, said, "Be the change you want to see in the world."

From the Better Days workbook passage 'Creating Change': "I say that first I must change myself into the person I want to be."

The words from the passage 'Creating Change' and Mahatma Gandhi indicate that by learning to focus on our personal experience of growth and change in the direction of our own interest, the world, will change in our direction, as we model the behaviors we want to see in the world.

Many programs say that giving back and helping others with the same problems as we have experienced is a sort of final step. Many people who have been successful in Recovery say that **giving back, taking commitments to support others,** and **remembering that they are an example of recovery in their communities** helped them the most in their recovery.

The reasoning of this program and in Peer Support in general is that showing recovery is possible occurs alongside every stage in the process and our actions create a lasting impact.

Stages of Wellness and Recovery:

Stage one
1 - Learning about recovery
2 - Exercising choice
3 - Seeking services i.e. counseling, therapy, medication, detox, peer support
4 - Staying away from harmful behaviors
5 - Staying away from negative influences, places or people
6 - Ending the pattern of isolation
7 - Finding positive role models
8 - Learning to ask for support
9 - Becoming personally responsible
10 - Experiencing joy and distress that can be overwhelming at times (extreme but fickle)

Stage 2
1 - Increase in physical health
2 - Ability to distinguish between different feelings and handle them
3 - Reducing emotions that interfere with our wellbeing
4 - Changes in thoughts, feelings and beliefs
5 - Zoning in on negative behaviors
6 - Having experienced the benefits of recovery, becoming committed to recovery

Stage 3
1 - Desire to make amends for harm we caused before we began recovery
2 - Becoming the "change we want to see in the world"
3 - Learning not to inflict self-harm or create hardship
4 - Developing honest and trusting relationships with more people

Stage 4
1 - Ability to use our strengths & knowledge to seize opportunities
2 - Automatic use of wellness tools and coping skills
3 - Self-forgiveness
4 - Building loving relationships rather than dependent ones
5 - Experiencing enduring happiness

Stage 5
1 - Becoming Self-actualized
2 - Gaining confidence, gratitude, and acceptance
3 - Developing integrity and humility
4 - Significant reduction of fear

Stage 6 - Celebration & Maintenance

The 10 Guiding Principles of Recovery

Taken From SAMHSA

Hope – belief that recovery is possible. When Hope is internalized and promoted by others, it is a key driver of recovery.

Person-driven – People define their own goals and the path to reaching them. Noone achieves them for us.

Many Pathways/Roads – Recovery is highly personalized and different for each person.

Holistic – Recovery emphasizes mind, body, spirit, and community.

Peer Support – Peers encourage and engage each other.

Relational – Recovery is supported by people who believe in a person's ability to recover.

Culture – Traditions, beliefs, and values are important in defining a person's recovery journey and path.

Trauma-informed – Support should promote safety and trust, creating choice, empowerment, and collaboration.

Strengths & Responsibilities – Individuals, communities, and families have strengths and resources that can benefit recovery. Individuals have the responsibility for their own recovery, but family and community support are essential.

Respect – acceptance and appreciation are key to recovery. This includes respect from other people and a respect for ourselves that help us develop a positive identity and confidence.

What Mentors Should Do

- Identify personal issues that negatively impact one's ability to perform mentor duties and perform appropriate self care before assisting others further.
- Utilize consultation regarding dual relationships.
- Utilize de-escalation techniques and educate individuals on suicide prevention concepts.
- Partner with the individual to access recovery-oriented services and supports
- Support the individual to identify options and participate in decisions connected to creating and completing recovery goals.
- Promote a wellness-focused approach to recovery.
- Utilize supervision and consultation regarding harm to self and others.
- Respond appropriately to personal stressors, triggers and indicators.
- Utilize trauma-informed care approaches.
- Assess the mentee's satisfaction with his/her progress toward recovery goals.

What Mentors Should Do

- Participate as a member of the individual's treatment team.
- Guarantee that recovery is based on the individual's strengths and resiliencies.
- Support the individual in defining spirituality on their own terms.
- Assist others to develop problem-solving skills.
- Assure that relationships, services and supports, reflect individual differences and cultural diversity.
- Support the individual's use of self-determination.
- Model acceptance and cultural humility.
- Partner with individuals to assist them in identifying their strengths, challenges to recovery and recovery capital.
- Apply Motivational Interviewing to assist individuals in during stages of change.
- Inform individuals of their options related to decisions that affect their recovery.

What Mentors Should Know

- System Level Advocacy – Advocating for changes to rules, policies, or laws that affect how someone lives their lives.

- Self Advocacy – Because very few people will advocate for us, and because recovery is person-driven, self-advocacy, the process of explaining why you deserve or are qualified for something, is the foundation for a strong recovery.

- Shared decision making – This is the process of a supporter and the person being supported collaborating to develop action plans that are agreed to by both partys.

- Person centered language – Instead of saying "he is an addict", say "name* is a person with an addiction. Instead of saying "they are Bipolar", say "name* is a person diagnosed with Bipolar." Instead of saying "they are a patient", say "name* is a person who is receiving services." Instead of saying "Bro", "Dude", or "Man", say "name*."

What Mentors Should Know

Navigating Services - Mentors will regularly require the services of other professionals to provide support and often make recommendations and referrals for other services. A mentor makes meaningful connections with many local services and leaders. Knowing when to say we don't have all the answers is an important characteristic of a mentor. Finding other providers of services who understand the significance of recovery and wellness versus treatment, and the specific needs for people facing specific challenges is encouraged.

Advocating for Recovery-Oriented Systems involves knowing the organization and leaders of the systems in your area on a deep level. We should develop close relationships with people who might provide recovery services to the people we serve. These deep relationships will inform us if the provider has a recovery-oriented mindset for which to advocate. A Recovery Oriented System of Care is a network of community-based services that meet the total needs of the person in recovery or their families. This includes emotional, occupational, educational, financial, spiritual, physical health, social, and environmental needs.

NOTES:

VIRTUES & VALUES

Please circle each value you feel describes who you are. Reflect on if you hold these values in high regard and what it means to you to posses this value. Consider if the values you didn't circle are important to you and determine what it would look like for you to posses that value and how you can incorporate it into your lifestyle. Try to be <u>as honest with yourself as you can during this exercise.</u> This is not an extensive list.

Orderliness	Generosity	Courage	Wisdom
Justice	Self-control	Assertiveness	Helpfulness
Modesty Peacefulness	Service	Forgiveness	
Purposefulness	Good Counsel	Responsibility	
Kindness Honesty	Respect	Tolerance	
Perseverance	Good judgment	Gratitude	Humility
Obedience Patience	Leadership/Command		
Truthfulness	Moderation	Loyalty	Courtesy
Friendliness	Sincerity	Prayerfulness	
Greatness/Magnanimity	Docility	Industriousness	
Foresight Patriotism			
Meekness Tact			

CHARACTER DEFECTS

Please circle each character defect you feel describes who you are. Reflect on your thoughts about the defects you circled. Determine if you would like to make a change to improve in these areas. <u>Try to be as honest with yourself as you can during this exercise.</u> This is not an extensive list.

Resentment	Cowardice	Self-Pity
Self-Justification	Self-Importance	Self-Condemnation
Lying and Evasiveness	Impatience	Hate
False Pride	Jealousy	Envy
Laziness	Procrastination	Insincerity
Negative Thinking	Immoral Thinking	Perfectionism
Criticizing	Greed	Distrustfulness
Hypochondria	Being Thin-Skinned	Moodiness
Being a Buzzkill	Willful Ignorance	callousness
Cruelty	Violence	Rigidity
Diffidence	Lechery	Self-Indulgence
Being a Know-It-All	Naiveté	Immaturity
Fastidiousness	Being overly picky	Prejudice
Rudeness	Crassness	

Note: You can use the pages with lines to add extra action steps that can't be fit into the colored tables.

"What I do in the 168 hours of the week."
Be as specific as possible, have at least 1 activity for every line, you can do multiple activities at the same time.

_____
_____
_____
_____
_____
_____
_____
_____
_____
_____
_____
_____
_____

Year 1 – Everyday Goals

Goal #1 _____

_____

Strengths & Recovery Capital	Obstacles	Action Steps	Date of Completion

Goal #1
Goal Description

_____

Action Steps

- _____
  _____
  _____

- _____
  _____
  _____

- _____
  _____
  _____

- _____
  _____
  _____

- _____
  _____
  _____

- People

  Involved_____

  _____

- _____

  _____

Year 1 – Everyday Goals

Goal #2 _____

_____

Strengths & Recovery Capital	Obstacles	Action Steps	Date of Completion

Goal #2
Goal Description

_____

Action Steps

- _____

  _____

- _____

  _____

- _____

  _____

- _____

  _____

- _____

  _____

- People

  Involved_____

  _____

- _____

  _____

Year 1 – Everyday Goals

Goal #3 _____

_____

Strengths & Recovery Capital	Obstacles	Action Steps	Date of Completion

Goal #3
Goal Description
_____

Action Steps

- _____
  _____

- _____
  _____
  _____

- _____
  _____

- _____
  _____

- _____
  _____

- People
  Involved_____
  _____

- _____
  _____

Year 1 – Everyday Goals

Goal #4 _____

_____

Strengths & Recovery Capital	Obstacles	Action Steps	Date of Completion

Goal #4
Goal Description

_____

Action Steps

- _____

  _____

- _____

  _____

  _____

- _____

  _____

- _____

  _____

- _____

  _____

- People

  Involved_____

  _____

- _____

  _____

Year 1 – Goals We Need Once in a While

Goal #5 _____

_____

Goal #5
Goal Description
_____

Action Steps

- _____

   _____

- _____

   _____

- _____

   _____

- _____

   _____

- _____

   _____

- People

   Involved_____

   _____

- _____

   _____

Year 1 – Goals We Need Once in a While

Goal #6 _____

_____

Goal #6
Goal Description

_____

Action Steps

- _____
  _____

- _____
  _____

- _____
  _____

- _____
  _____

- _____
  _____

- People

  Involved_____

  _____

- _____

  _____

Year 1 – Goals We Need Once in a While

Goal #7 _____

_____

Goal #7
Goal Description

_____

Action Steps

- _____

  _____

- _____

  _____

- _____

  _____

- _____

  _____

- _____

  _____

- People

  Involved_____

  _____

- _____

  _____

Year 1 – Big Achievements

Goal #8 _____

_____

Strengths & Recovery Capital	Obstacles	Action Steps	Date of Completion

Goal #8
Goal Description

_____

Action Steps

- _____

  _____

- _____

  _____

  _____

- _____

  _____

- _____

  _____

- _____

  _____

- People

  Involved_____

  _____

- _____

  _____

Year 1 – Big Achievements

Goal #9 _____

_____

Strengths & Recovery Capital	Obstacles	Action Steps	Date of Completion

Goal #9
Goal Description
_____

Action Steps

- _____

 _____

- _____

 _____

- _____

 _____

- _____

 _____

- _____

 _____

- People

 Involved_____

 _____

- _____

 _____

Year 1 – Big Achievements

Goal #10
_____

_____

Strengths & Recovery Capital	Obstacles	Action Steps	Date of Completion

Goal #10
Goal Description

_____

Action Steps

- _____

  _____

- _____

  _____

- _____

  _____

- _____

  _____

- _____

  _____

- People

  Involved_____

  _____

- _____

  _____

Year 1 – Big Achievements

Goal #11

_____

_____

Strengths & Recovery Capital	Obstacles	Action Steps	Date of Completion

Goal #11
Goal Description
_____

Action Steps

- _____

  _____

- _____

  _____

- _____

  _____

- _____

  _____

- _____

  _____

- People

  Involved_____

  _____

- _____

  _____

Year 1 – Big Achievements

Goal #12
_____
_____

Strengths & Recovery Capital	Obstacles	Action Steps	Date of Completion

Goal #12
Goal Description
_____

Action Steps

- _____

  _____

- _____

  _____

- _____

  _____

- _____

  _____

- _____

  _____

- People

  Involved_____

  _____

- _____

  _____

Year 1 – Big Achievements

Goal #13
_____

_____

Strengths & Recovery Capital	Obstacles	Action Steps	Date of Completion

Goal #13
Goal Description
_____

Action Steps

- _____
  _____

- _____
  _____
  _____

- _____
  _____

- _____
  _____

- _____
  _____

- People

  Involved_____

  _____

- _____

  _____

Year 1 – Big Achievements

Goal #14

_____

_____

Strengths & Recovery Capital	Obstacles	Action Steps	Date of Completion

Goal #14
Goal Description

_____

Action Steps

- _____
  _____

- _____
  _____

- _____
  _____

- _____
  _____

- _____
  _____

- People Involved _____
  _____

- _____
  _____

Note: You can use the pages with lines to add extra action steps that can't be fit into the colored tables.

3 year – Everyday Goals

Goal #1 _____

_____

Strengths & Recovery Capital	Obstacles	Action Steps	Date of Completion

Goal #1
Goal Description
_____

Action Steps

- _____

  _____

- _____

  _____

- _____

  _____

- _____

  _____

- _____

  _____

- People

  Involved_____

  _____

- _____

  _____

3 year– Everyday Goals

Goal #2 _____

_____

Strengths & Recovery Capital	Obstacles	Action Steps	Date of Completion

Goal #2
Goal Description
_____

Action Steps

- _____

  _____

- _____

  _____

- _____

  _____

- _____

  _____

- _____

  _____

- People

  Involved_____

  _____

- _____

  _____

3 year– Everyday Goals

Goal #3 _____

_____

Strengths & Recovery Capital	Obstacles	Action Steps	Date of Completion

Goal #3
Goal Description
_____

Action Steps

- _____
  _____

- _____
  _____

- _____
  _____

- _____
  _____

- _____
  _____

- People

  Involved_____

  _____

- _____
  _____

3 year– Everyday Goals

Goal #4 _____

_____

Strengths & Recovery Capital	Obstacles	Action Steps	Date of Completion

Goal #4
Goal Description
_____

Action Steps

- _____

  _____

- _____

  _____

- _____

  _____

- _____

  _____

- _____

  _____

- People

  Involved_____

  _____

- _____

  _____

3 year– Goals We Need Once in a While

Goal #5 _____

_____

Strengths & Recovery Capital	Obstacles	Action Steps	Date of Completion

Goal #5
Goal Description
_____

Action Steps

- _____

  _____

- _____

  _____

- _____

  _____

- _____

  _____

- _____

  _____

- People

  Involved_____

  _____

- _____

  _____

3 year– Goals We Need Once in a While

Goal #6 _____

_____

Strengths & Recovery Capital	Obstacles	Action Steps	Date of Completion

Goal #6
Goal Description
_____

Action Steps

- _____

  _____

- _____

  _____

- _____

  _____

- _____

  _____

- _____

  _____

- People

  Involved_____

  _____

- _____

  _____

3 year– Goals We Need Once in a While

Goal #7 _____

_____

Strengths & Recovery Capital	Obstacles	Action Steps	Date of Completion

Goal #7
Goal Description
_____

Action Steps

- _____

  _____

- _____

  _____

- _____

  _____

- _____

  _____

- _____

  _____

- People

  Involved_____

  _____

- _____

  _____

3 year– Big Achievements

Goal #8 _____

_____

Strengths & Recovery Capital	Obstacles	Action Steps	Date of Completion

Goal #8
Goal Description
_____

Action Steps

- _____

  _____

- _____

  _____

- _____

  _____

- _____

  _____

- _____

  _____

- People

  Involved_____

  _____

- _____

  _____

3 year– Big Achievements

Goal #9 _____

_____

Strengths & Recovery Capital	Obstacles	Action Steps	Date of Completion

Goal #9
Goal Description

_____

Action Steps

- _____
  _____

- _____
  _____

- _____
  _____

- _____
  _____

- _____
  _____

- People

  Involved_____

  _____

- _____
  _____

3 year– Big Achievements

Goal #10

_____

_____

Strengths & Recovery Capital	Obstacles	Action Steps	Date of Completion

Goal #10
Goal Description
_____

Action Steps

- _____

  _____

- _____

  _____

- _____

  _____

- _____

  _____

- _____

  _____

- People

  Involved_____

  _____

- _____

  _____

3 year– Big Achievements

Goal #11

_____

_____

Strengths & Recovery Capital	Obstacles	Action Steps	Date of Completion

Goal #11
Goal Description
_____

Action Steps

- _____

  _____

- _____

  _____

- _____

  _____

- _____

  _____

- _____

  _____

- People

  Involved_____

  _____

- _____

  _____

3 year– Big Achievements

Goal #12

_____

_____

Strengths & Recovery Capital	Obstacles	Action Steps	Date of Completion

Goal #12
Goal Description
_____

Action Steps

- _____

  _____

- _____

  _____

- _____

  _____

- _____

  _____

- _____

  _____

- People

  Involved_____

  _____

- _____

  _____

3 year– Big Achievements

Goal #13

_____

_____

Strengths & Recovery Capital	Obstacles	Action Steps	Date of Completion

Goal #13
Goal Description
_____

Action Steps

- _____

  _____

- _____

  _____

- _____

  _____

- _____

  _____

- _____

  _____

- People

  Involved_____

  _____

- _____

  _____

3 year– Big Achievements

Goal #14

_____

_____

Strengths & Recovery Capital	Obstacles	Action Steps	Date of Completion

Goal #14
Goal Description
_____

Action Steps

- _____

  _____

- _____

  _____

- _____

  _____

- _____

  _____

- _____

  _____

- People Involved_____

  _____

- _____

  _____

Note: You can use the pages with lines to add extra action steps that can't be fit into the colored tables.

5 Year – Everyday Goals

Goal #1 _____

_____

Strengths & Recovery Capital	Challenges	Action Steps	Date of Completion

Goal #1
Goal Description

_____

Action Steps

- _____
  _____

- _____
  _____
  _____

- _____
  _____

- _____
  _____

- _____
  _____

- People Involved_____
  _____

- _____
  _____

5 Year – Everyday Goals

Goal #2 _____

_____

Strengths & Recovery Capital	Challenges	Action Steps	Date of Completion

Goal #2
Goal Description
_____

Action Steps

- _____

  _____

- _____

  _____

- _____

  _____

- _____

  _____

- _____

  _____

- People

  Involved_____

  _____

- _____

  _____

5 Year– Everyday Goals

Goal #3 _____

_____

Strengths & Recovery Capital	Challenges	Action Steps	Date of Completion

Goal #3
Goal Description

_____

Action Steps

- _____
  _____

- _____
  _____

- _____
  _____

- _____
  _____

- _____
  _____

- People

  Involved_____

  _____

- _____

  _____

5 Year– Everyday Goals

Goal #4 _____

_____

Strengths & Recovery Capital	Challenges	Action Steps	Date of Completion

Goal #4
Goal Description
_____

Action Steps

- _____

  _____

- _____

  _____

- _____

  _____

- _____

  _____

- _____

  _____

- People

  Involved_____

  _____

- _____

  _____

5 Year– Goals We Need Once in a While

Goal #5 _____

_____

Goal #5
Goal Description
_____

Action Steps

- _____
  _____
  _____

- _____
  _____
  _____

- _____
  _____
  _____

- _____
  _____
  _____

- _____
  _____
  _____

- People Involved_____
  _____

- _____
  _____

5 Year – Goals We Need Once in a While

Goal #6 _____

_____

Goal #6
Goal Description

_____

Action Steps

- _____

  _____

- _____

  _____

- _____

  _____

- _____

  _____

- _____

  _____

- People

  Involved_____

  _____

- _____

  _____

5 Year – Goals We Need Once in a While

Goal #7 _____

_____

Strengths & Recovery Capital	Challenges	Action Steps	Date of Completion

Goal #7
Goal Description
_____

Action Steps

- _____

  _____

- _____

  _____

- _____

  _____

- _____

  _____

- _____

  _____

- People

  Involved_____

  _____

- _____

  _____

5 Year – Big Achievements

Goal #8 _____

_____

Strengths & Recovery Capital	Challenges	Action Steps	Date of Completion

Goal #8
Goal Description
_____

Action Steps

- _____
  _____

- _____
  _____

- _____
  _____

- _____
  _____

- _____
  _____

- People

  Involved_____

  _____

- _____

  _____

5 Year – Big Achievements

Goal #9 _____

_____

Strengths & Recovery Capital	Challenges	Action Steps	Date of Completion

Goal #9
Goal Description
_____

Action Steps

- _____

  _____

- _____

  _____

- _____

  _____

- _____

  _____

- _____

  _____

- People

  Involved_____

  _____

- _____

  _____

5 Year – Big Achievements

Goal #10
_____ _____
_____

Strengths & Recovery Capital	Challenges	Action Steps	Date of Completion

_____

5 Year– Big Achievements

Goal #11

_____

_____

Strengths & Recovery Capital	Challenges	Action Steps	Date of Completion

Goal #11
Goal Description
_____

Action Steps

- _____

  _____

- _____

  _____

  _____

- _____

  _____

- _____

  _____

- _____

  _____

- People

  Involved_____

  _____

- _____

  _____

5 Year – Big Achievements

Goal #12

_____

_____

Strengths & Recovery Capital	Challenges	Action Steps	Date of Completion

Goal #12
Goal Description
_____

Action Steps

- _____

  _____

- _____

  _____

  _____

- _____

  _____

- _____

  _____

- _____

  _____

- People

  Involved_____

  _____

- _____

  _____

5 Year – Big Achievements

Goal #13

_____

_____

Strengths & Recovery Capital	Challenges	Action Steps	Date of Completion

Goal #13
Goal Description

_____

Action Steps

- _____
  _____

- _____
  _____

- _____
  _____

- _____
  _____

- _____
  _____

- People

  Involved_____

  _____

- _____

  _____

5 Year – Big Achievements

Goal #14

_____

_____

Strengths & Recovery Capital	Challenges	Action Steps	Date of Completion

Goal #14
Goal Description
_____

Action Steps

- _____

  _____

- _____

  _____

- _____

  _____

- _____

  _____

- _____

  _____

- People

  Involved_____

  _____

- _____

  _____

Facilitation Process

Level 1 Groups – Co-facilitator Required*

The slides that can be read in the workbook or PowerPoint will be divided between all those wishing to receive a certificate of participation or completion, including participation from the facilitators. The Facilitators will start by explaining why we request full participation and the reward of either a certificate of completion or participation. The Information on participation requirements is on page two underneath the table of contents.

The Facilitators will read the first two slides of the first presentation. After that, all slides will be divided up between the participants. The exceptions to this are the slides in the first session's presentation following the slide title "Why We Present the Recovery Fundamentals and Parallel Recovery Concepts in this Order." These slides sometimes contain more than one Fundamental or Concept and there will be a different reader for each of these.

At the end of each session, the Facilitator will read the last slide that conveys information related to the upcoming session. After this, the remainder of the time will be spent on open discussion of the day's session. For session one this will be the full span of 2 hours, for the remaining session it will be the span of 3 hours.

The remaining sessions also have sections titled 'How does this passage connect or relate to the concept or fundamental.' These questions entail a short response that should connect the passage read just before this question to the Recovery Concept or Fundamental being discussed at the time. Everyone has the capability to answer these questions so everyone desiring a certificate of participation or completion will answer these including the facilitator, unless facilitator participation means some participants will not have the chance to participate.

Participation points will not be lost for these questions if there were not enough questions for everyone to get a chance to participate. A participation sheet will be provided which specifies how many participation points a person will need in each category of participation. For those who have not had a chance to answer these questions, they will have an opportunity to revisit them at the end of the group.

Sessions 2 – 5 also have many short questions. There are usually 3 questions for each passage. These are divided between all those seeking a certificate of completion and the Facilitators. These questions are not required to be answered by those seeking a certificate of participation.

The Facilitator will not participate or read unless there are fewer than 5 people attempting a certificate of completion, in which case, only participating when they have the least amount of participation compared to those seeking a certificate. Participants can choose when they would like to participate in order to get the right amount of participation points, however when some of them are close to full points, the facilitator will begin asking specific people to participate if a participant has the least amount of participation.

If participants do not have a response to a particular question, the Facilitator will step in and answer the question. If participants did not get enough participation points from this question-and-answer section, we can allow them to answer other questions from the session at the end as a revisitation.

To revisit a question requires them to have completed enough of their answers to share them and receive the required completion points. This might be useful for participants that did not complete enough of their questions before the group where the questions they did answer in the book were answered by other participants. Even if the participant did not complete a question before group, we can allow them to develop a quick answer on the spot if they are able.

Once the presentation process is over for the session, we allow the rest of the time to be open discussion starting with the facilitator asking the group if they have any questions, allowing participants to ask questions here. Next, we will do a check in, asking the group how they are doing with the concepts or fundamentals covered in the session. Once 2 hours have elapsed for session one, or three hours for all other sessions, the session is complete.

This is how the group will be Facilitated.

Continuum Groups – Level 2 Group

The continuum groups are meant for people who have already participated in a regular group and who have a desire to participate in a longer-term group. Also, in cases where a Facilitator does not have a Co-facilitator, they can provide Continuum Groups instead. If a Co-facilitator is available, we should always try to do the level 1 group first so that people who want either of the two certificates can get them and they can receive a reward or token from the group in the form of a certificate of participation (not of completion) or a coin (coins which we will make soon.) Level 2 groups will also provide a certificate or coin, however only after 52 sessions have been completed.

In this type of group, the Facilitator does not need to discuss participation requirements. Also, the first session will be given out as a packet of paper to any participants attending the group for the first time. By doing this, we skip session 1 and actually present material starting with session 2.

Sessions 2-5 will be broken down into 3 groups apiece. Instead of presenting all of the material for session 2, we will present the material for the concepts of Self-care, Recovery Planning, and Mentorship on three different days. We will separate the fundamentals from sessions 3-5 in the same way, tackling them in three days rather than in one.

The participants do not need to bring their books or read any slides. In this version of the group, the Facilitator reads everything. There is the introduction material starting with each concept or fundamental, followed by an inspirational passage, followed by asking the question "How does this passage relate to the 'concept' or 'fundamental.'

In asking this question, in the level 1 group, we like everyone to have already answered this question in their books and to read their response for the group. In this case, we ask them to answer the question spontaneously with the thoughts they have at the moment. This should ensure that even if they answer the question similarly each time, they may have noticed a connection today different from what they wrote in their books or answered in a previous level 2 group.

After this question, there are generally 3 questions asked that relate to the passage or recovery in general. These questions will also be answered spontaneously without the use of their book. These questions are usually something that they have experienced in more than one way and can provide different answers to each time they come across them.

Level 2 groups are meant to be an hour long. If the group runs shorter than this period, facilitators can do a check-in, asking how participants are experiencing the concept or fundamental in their lives. This group is meant to be continuous, thus the word Continuum in the name. While we will present the material in 12 weeks, people may want to continue them longer because with new participants being added consistently there should be diversity in how people answer questions over time.

This is how the group should be operated.

How to Become an RRPS Facilitator

To become an RRPS Facilitator, you must first, participate in an RRPS group. You cannot become a Facilitator for each of the different groups by only participating in one type of group. In order to qualify as a Facilitator of a specific group, a potential Facilitator has to participate in that specific group and earn a certificate of completion.

There are three different programs or groups. Radical Recovery Peer Support (RRPS), RRPS-University, and RRPS-Liberation. RRPS is for people who are experiencing general distress.

RRPS-University is for people experiencing distress but who are either attempting a form of education beyond k-12, or who are thinking about doing so. RRPS-Liberation is for people with a criminal history that includes Driving Under the Influence.

At the present time, RRPS liberation training is only for potential Facilitators who have a criminal record or whose criminal records were expunged or pardoned. In the future, anyone can become an RRPS-Liberation Facilitator if they know another RRPS-Liberation facilitator, believe that the program is helping people with criminal records, and receive a written recommendation from an RRPS-Liberation Facilitator stating they believe you have the ability to work well with participants of this background or that they can attest that you have worked with this group of people before. For people that do not have criminal records who receive the ability to facilitate groups, they will only need to earn a certificate of participation instead of a certificate of completion.

For RRPS-University, a Facilitator must show proof that they have at least 25 credits of college experience, or that they have received a certification in a particular skill and have worked in that field for 3 years.

For the RRPS program specifically, other than RRPS-University or RRPS-Liberation, there are no background requirements to become a Facilitator.

*After personally participating in a group, the Facilitation training will begin. Facilitation training involves working with an Advanced Level Co-Facilitator to present a group to 3 people (no more than 3). They will do this on a recorded Zoom session so the recording can be viewed to make sure the presentation process went smoothly. The low number of participants will ensure that the facilitator will also participate, as participation is divided among the participants and the Facilitators when the number of people attempting a certificate of completion is less than 5 persons.

For more information on how to divide the participation during a regular (non-training group) consult the text on page two of the Facilitator handbook. Or check out our blog titled "Participation Requirements" at www.communitypeerservices.com/blog This blog also states the amount of completion of the workbook needed by each person attempting to become a Facilitator.

During training, the potential Facilitator is not required to examine participants workbooks for completeness, this will be for their Advanced Level Co-facilitator to complete.

A potential Facilitator may need to find participants for their training group. We cannot guarantee that we will have willing participants. This means a Facilitator in training must find three people who want to get certified. We suggest trying to network with others in the mental health recovery, substance use recovery, or criminal Reentry fields such as Peer Supporters, or Forensic Peer Supporters via your social media.

The fee for participation in a group is $187.50 and the fee for the training opportunity is also $187.5. Payment plans are available upon request but for a higher overall price of $250.00 divided among 52 weeks. Anyone who does not pay their payment plans on time will have their certifications suspended. This means that they will not be able to provide certificates of completion that will be accepted by us, which means that the people participating in a group with a Facilitator who has been suspended will not be able to become facilitators and will need to do the group with a facilitator who is current with their payments.

**Once a person participates in a Facilitator training program, they are qualified to Facilitate any group without having to run a practice group for each (as long as background requirements are met). However, they will need to earn a certificate of completion for each group they want to Facilitate. Facilitator certification is only valid for 3 years. Every three years Facilitators must participate in their choice of group. Also, for the first 6 years Facilitators will have to do a video presntation every 3 years.

Author's note:

Hi, I am Dakota Fisher.

I designed this group because I believe in recovery. This will probably not be the only tool in your recovery toolbox, because a toolbox that has only one tool in it usually doesn't have much value. I hope that people participating in this program develop a system of recovery that works for them.

There are many systems of recovery that I participate in because my mind needs continual education concerning the issues I face. With respect to educating myself on these issues, I know that 1000 programs might never be enough to relieve me of an insanity that had at one time completely overtaken my ability to function productively and happily in society and my community.

My beliefs, thoughts, and feelings became twisted in a way that I could not see anything of value in the world and had become hopeless. No tool that I discovered had a complete answer because all of them were made by people who have different and unique views on recovery and had different experiences that helped them become thoughtful in specific areas.

Because no one has an exact recipe for how to help you recover, as only you can discover the mix of thoughts, beliefs, and feelings that work for you, it might be hard to find what is needed to begin and complete your recovery journey. In the worst instances, some of the people or programs we reach out to for help will try to convince us that their program is the best and that we should pick one above the others and commit to it.

From my perspective, one of the most important things in my recovery was not the programs themselves, but the people I would meet in a program that would become part of my support group. Having these people in my life helps me stay open-minded; moreover, it ensures that I usually have someone in recovery around me at all times, and if not, they are only a phone call away.

The way I see it, I need a diverse group of supporters, because each person in my circle only knows the part of the picture that they have experienced or been exposed to. A lot of times, people who are very knowledgeable about one thing do not have any valid answers to certain problems I have experienced. So, if one person doesn't have an answer, I need to find someone who does. This can only be accomplished by meeting them where they are at, wherever they are at.

In some cases, I will find that I can't entirely agree with a particular philosophy, or that a person who is supposed to be providing me with aid does not understand where I am coming from or why I feel the way I feel. I might sometimes be considering finding a new supporter. When this happens, I do not curse the whole program or field of care because of my bad experience. Most of the resources out there provide value to many people, or else they would not survive.

Therefore, it is important for me to carefully consider what it is about a program or person that I am in disagreement with and see if there is another option that will provide me with the best benefits that that program, service, or person offers. This might require a searching and fearless education into recovery resources to find out about their purpose, and their promises.

If I feel like something is not to my liking or is adversely affecting me, I want to have supporters, or trusted friends or family members who I can ask if they have noticed unpleasant changes or if they think I've been doing better. Sometimes it is hard for me to tell because I have had many intermingling problems that clouded my judgement. Having these people around will allow us to bring them to our appointments and explain what they are seeing in such cases where we want a change to be made but the person we are relying on to make the change doesn't listen to us or believe we are seeing clearly.

So, this program and education are both tools we might want in our toolbox. Other important "tools" or "resources" are having an open mind and having a willingness to experience new things. Open-mindedness and willingness will allow us to take advantage of the good aspects of any program and leave behind what doesn't work for us.

As a final note, one of the most pervasive and underlying concepts of this program is mentorship. The difference between mentorship and sponsorship is not so evident at first glance, but there are some distinguishing features. Sponsors of certain programs are indeed meant to practice the principles they have learned in all areas of their lives, but most people in this position will not be sponsors at work, school, or public places. They reserve their sponsorship for people with the particular issues that underlie their program of choice. A sponsor will usually not discuss issues that are outside of their primary area of concern. Some sponsors will say ambiguously that if we refrain from harmful behaviors everything will fall into place.

A Mentor will be a mentor in all places and for any issue. Mentors exhibit the best version of themselves in the work they do, in their field of study, in social and recreational settings, etc... Because we never know where we will meet a person that needs our help, we will try to live to our fullest potential so that when a person asks us how we handle situations with such grace, or where we find our motivation, we can tell them. Living our fullest potential will attract people to our way of life. Mentors will also be willing to talk about any facet of life with a person who is struggling even if they are not the best resource for that particular concern and will try to connect the person to someone with more insights if they find they cannot offer meaningful aid. We are always mentors, and our behavior will influence people for good or bad whether we know it does or not.

Authors Background

United States Army Veteran

BS Finance (honors)

Current MBA student

Pennsylvania - Certified Peer Specialist

Forensic Peer Specialist

MRT Facilitator

Mental Health First Aider

**Formerly Incarcerated Person*

References

- King, M. L., Jr. (1967, October 26). What Is Your Life's Blueprint? Barratt Junior High School in Philadelphia, Pennsylvania.
- King Jr., M. L. (1965, March 25). Keep Moving from This Mountain [Speech]. Spelman College, Atlanta, Georgia.

Experience the Insight.

"Personal experiences and insights on recovery from a person in recovery – Innovative mental health workbooks that ask us insightful questions that help us make sense of complex issues of life."

www.communitypeerservices.com |

Experience the Insight.

"Personal experiences and insights on recovery from a person in recovery – Innovative mental health workbooks that ask us insightful questions that help us make sense of complex issues of life."

www.communitypeerservices.com

Radical Recovery Peer Support

Community & Peer Services
Caps

Community & Peer Services
Caps

Community & Peer Services
Caps

To Explore Our Website go to

www.communitypeerservices.com

To learn more about our different group or training programs visit

www.communitypeerservices.com/blog

Find us on:
Facebook @ Community and Peer Services
LinkedIn @ Community and Peer Services
Twitter @2023caps
Reddit @ #RadicalRecovery
YouTube @ #RadicalRecovery